Teaching the Three Rs

Through Movement Experiences

A HANDBOOK FOR TEACHERS

Anne Green Gilbert

The University of Washington
Seattle, Washington

Burgess Publishing Company
Minneapolis, Minnesota

Consulting Editors to the Publisher

Eloise M. Jaeger
University of Minnesota
Minneapolis, Minnesota

Robert M. Clayton
Colorado State University
Fort Collins, Colorado

Copyright © 1977 by Burgess Publishing Company
Printed in the United States of America
Library of Congress Catalog Card Number 76-19465
ISBN 0-8087-0751-5

0 9 8 7 6 5 4 3

Photographs by Howard R. Giske
Book and cover design by Barbara Warrington

Dedicated to my husband and son, David and Huw Anthony Gilbert, who gave me the encouragement and time to write this book, and to my father and mother, Dwight and Barbara Green, who gave me the education and confidence.

Preface

The writing of this book has been a desire of mine since I first taught third grade in a North Chicago elementary school. We had all the new textbooks, language arts kits, science kits, and math games, but the children still were not motivated or excited about learning. They sat at their desks all day long, swallowing and regurgitating facts. Freedom of movement was allowed only during recess, which was always bedlam from the explosion of all their pent-up energies. I was disturbed by the students' lack of motivation, creativity, and maturity. Being a dancer and dance educator and realizing the importance and values of non-verbal communication, I decided to start a movement program in my classroom. I hoped this would help the attitudes of my students.

The change was amazing! The excitement generated from being allowed to move more freely in the classroom helped rather than hindered class control. Instead of the occassional fights caused by the frustration of sitting all day, there was an atmosphere of cooperation. Thirty children cannot move around each other and thirty desks without learning the art of cooperation! The scores on their spelling tests greatly improved after sessions in body spelling. The children took a new interest in math after making up problems with their bodies. They understood the revolutions of the planets after moving around the classroom in the solar systems they had created. Recess became a time for more creative problem solving through movement instead of brawling chaos.

I could go on and on because the changes were so exciting, but you will discover these changes for yourself if you employ movement experiences in your own classroom.

This book is geared for the classroom teacher (K-6) who has little or no experience in movement education. It can also be used to advantage by preschool teachers and physical or movement education specialists. It is a unique book on movement because it emphasizes the integration of movement with the academic subjects taught in the classroom. This book presents simple, clear activities for teaching language arts, mathematics, science, social studies, art, and music through movement.

It is my hope that these activities intrigue and excite you enough to employ movement experiences in your classroom. It always takes courage to try something new, especially when it involves not only allowing but encouraging your students to get out of their seats and to move joyously and freely around the room. But once you try this new method of teaching, I am sure that you will never restrict yourself solely to traditional methods again. You will find it as refreshing as your students do.

When you do introduce the various movement experiences into your classroom, I know that you and your students will think of many new exciting activities to add to those presented in this book. I would welcome hearing about your experiences. Any questions or problems you encounter may be addressed to me in care of the publisher. Good luck and have fun!

I would like to gratefully acknowledge Melissa Gloyd for her work on the bibliography, Howard R. Giske for his excellent photographs and easy going manner, Sandra T. Barckley for her help with typing the manuscript, Susan Gleason for her support, David Gilbert for his advice, the Bukoskeys for babysitting while I was working in the schools, Robert Lakemacher and Ann Seivert of Burgess Publishing Company for their faith and assistance and Judy O'Donnell for her excellent editing.

My thanks also go to the teachers and students at Richard Bennett Elementary School, Bellevue, Washington, for letting me share my ideas and photograph the results. Thanks particularly to Don Hultgren, Principal; Wanda Chillingworth, Chris Fliflet, Diane Della Cruz, and their first grade students; Joan Kenney and her third grade students; Don Jones, Jim Churchill, Norma Williams, and their sixth grade students. Lastly I would like to thank Amy, Benji, Hilary, Jory, Kathleen, Marcy, Nicole, and Rachel, some of the three- and four-year-olds I teach at Dance Theatre Seattle.

Fall 1976   A.G.G.

Contents

Introduction to Movement Experiences

INTRODUCTION
TO
MOVEMENT
EXPERIENCES

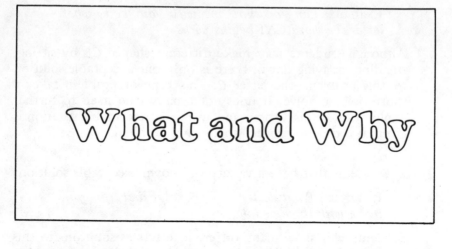

What and Why

What are movement experiences? Through the activities in this book, children experience movement by using non-verbal communication to solve problems in language arts, mathematics, science, social studies, art and music. They discover what their bodies are capable of doing. They experience freedom from inhibitions. They explore their academic world through movement.

These movement experiences are not meant to replace the traditional methods of teaching the *three Rs*. Instead, they should be used along with these methods to increase motivation and learning. Neither are they intended as a panacea for the variety of ills plaguing many of our schools. However, they will help make the teaching and learning of basic academic skills more enjoyable and meaningful for both teachers and students.

The movement experiences are presented to the children through specific problems that they solve by using their bodies in a variety of ways. Competitive games are not stressed. The problems are given to the children verbally or through the use of task sheets and cards. The problems can be solved individually, by partners, or by small and large groups. The movement problems are directly correlated to academic concepts, which is to say, there is a precise pairing of movement experiences with intellectual functions.

There are three different types of movement problems:

    1. Problems that have one known acceptable solution

Example: *Can you show me with your body what letter the word* CAT *begins with?*

Although students may make different shaped *C*'s by sitting, standing, or lying down, there is only one acceptable solution to this problem—the letter *C*. This type of problem takes a short time to solve. It does not usually lend itself to further exploration or discussion, and when the acceptable solution is given, it is time to proceed to another problem.

2. Problems that have a variety of known acceptable solutions

Example: *What letters of the alphabet can you make with three people?*

Students will show many different letters as solutions to this problem. In fact, all the letters of the alphabet can be made with three people, and the twenty-six letters represent the many acceptable solutions. This type of problem takes time to solve because there is more than one solution. It may lead to further exploration. After students have solved the problem, you may ask them to find other solutions. It may also lead to further discussion. For example, you might ask, "Are some letters easier to make with three people than with one or two? Why?"

3. Problems that have an infinite number of solutions to be identified or discovered

Examples: *Let us add new letters to our alphabet. Can you make a crazy letter with your body that no one has seen before and give it a name?*

Show me what shape the wind is.

Show me how the color red makes you feel.

Create your own planet and show me how it moves.

This type of problem highlights individuality as each student will have a unique solution. Any sincere solution is acceptable. The solutions are not known until the time of discovery. This type of problem may take the longest to solve because the students are entering into uncharted territory. They must rely on their creativity and ingenuity. You will discover that the more sophisticated students become in their movement language, the longer these problems will take to solve and the more complicated the answers will be. You may go into great depth in exploring the problems and their solutions. These problems often tap feelings and discussion of these feelings can have beneficial results.

Now that you have a better understanding of movement experiences as they pertain to this book, you may be asking yourself, "Why are movement experiences important to the growth and development of a child?" People's first means of communication was through movement. The spoken and written word came later. And yet, through the centuries in our society, movement for communication has become a specialized art form—dance—to be enjoyed by only a small group of trained individuals. The joy of expressing oneself freely through movement is not something that is experienced daily by many Americans. How far we have come from our beginnings, and what a sad price we pay for our sophistication.

We must free ourselves from our inhibitions regarding movement, and this can only be done through a change in our educational philosophy. In order to achieve this change, the values of non-verbal communication need to be made known.

Intellectual, physical, and emotional growth are stimulated through movement experiences. Children are given problems to solve. They must think of a solution or more often several solutions. The problems become more and more complex as the children become more experienced. Their minds and imaginations are continually challenged. They are also learning a new vocabulary and new principles of space, time, force, and flow.

Children solve these intellectual problems through movement, thereby stimulating their physical growth. The problems demand exacting physical solutions using all parts of the body. Working with movement experiences daily will help keep children physically fit. Furthermore, children learn all about their bodies through movement experiences. They learn the names of body parts, what these parts can do, and how these parts function. Children become aware of how to create energy and how to conserve it. They learn about tension and relaxation. They learn to understand physical strength and weakness. In short, they become familiar with their bodies so that they can better master them.

Working on the problems and their solutions brings forth emotions and feelings. The children are continually reacting to the problems, and these reactions are often revealed in discussions. Problems dealing with emotions and sensory perception are commonly undertaken. Because children are able to freely express their emotions, they can channel hostilities and frustrations in a harmless, creative way through movement experiences instead of through fighting.

Work in movement is an excellent way to release classroom tensions. In a very real sense, movement experiences integrate the mind, body, and soul of a person. This so rarely happens in any elementary school. The classroom teacher concentrates on intellectual growth, the physical educator on physical growth, and few pay attention to emotional growth. A teacher presenting movement experiences to students concentrates on all three areas and helps create a well-balanced total individual.

Experiences in movement exploration allow children the freedom to express themselves in non-verbal terms. This can be very important for the inarticulate child. There is a lot written in the popular press these days about body language. A person who is free to express himself or herself through movement certainly will be more sensitive to others' movements and their meanings, and ultimately, should be more understanding of others' moods and problems.

How many people you know immerse themselves in some physical activity while trying to solve an intellectual problem? If you have ever watched anybody pacing back and forth while trying to think, you must know that movement stimulates the brain. What better way to get children intellectually stimulated than by introducing movement experiences right in the classroom to help solve reading, writing, and arithmetic problems.

Movement exploration lends itself to individualized instruction. Each child uses his or her body to solve a problem. As no two bodies are alike, a teacher must look at students as individuals. Also, there can be as many different solutions to a problem as there are children. This will help point out people's individuality and thereby develop social awareness. The way people solve problems is not only dependent on their intelligence and creativity but also their backgrounds (race, culture, religion, environment). All of this can be brought forth in discussions after the solutions are shown. As a child works with partners in small groups and later in large groups, social awareness is developed. Each child must learn to work and cooperate with others to solve common problems. This can often be difficult and challenging, and cooperation is all too infrequently seen in elementary schools. Learning to cooperate will teach respect for others.

Every child working in movement experiences has success. There is no such thing as failure because each child proceeds at his or her own rate. Each child's solutions are accepted because there is no right or wrong way to explore movement. This continual success helps build a positive self-concept. Success can be so important to a child who has trouble in school, since self-respect is fostered through success. Soon a child who has been discouraged will begin to gain confidence in other areas as well as movement. If a child can solve math problems through movement, he or she will soon be enjoying math and gaining the confidence to use more traditional methods of learning. Solving problems successfully will build self-image, self-awareness, and self-direction.

Perhaps the most important reason that movement experience should be an integral part of the elementary school curriculum is the impetus it can have for learning. Piaget states that the stage of "concrete operations" is usually reached between the ages of seven and eleven. He recommends that the teacher provide a very *active* curriculum particularly early in this stage. Children at these ages need to work with and handle many concrete objects before they can readily understand abstract verbalization. Piaget also maintains that the key to learning is not to verbalize too much during the stage of "concrete operations." The child requires a great deal of physical activity. What better way to teach the academic subjects than through movement? What better concrete object to manipulate than the child's own body?

If children are not ready for abstract verbalization, use non-verbalization. If children work with their bodies to solve math problems, they will better understand the concepts involved when the teacher verbalizes them. They will not only understand the concepts better but will remember them longer, for when an intellectual exercise is combined with associated physical activity, the impression is more lasting.

Up to now I have been discussing the benefits of this type of program to the children involved. There are also benefits to teachers and parents.

Because the children solve problems through movement, the teacher receives immediate feedback. The teacher can tell whether the class understands a concept or whether more work in that area is needed. It's not necessary to grade papers to determine this. The teacher can also tell what individuals need personal attention. With the traditional method of question and answer, many children, who may or may not understand the concept being studied, go unnoticed. When all the children are involved in working out solutions at the same time, those children who have a firm grasp of the subject under study are immediately apparent to the teacher.

Parents will be happy to learn that the movement experiences presented in this book are a very inexpensive motivational and educational tool. There is no equipment to buy and no learning kits or books are necessary.

With all these benefits how can we have neglected movement experiences in our elementary schools for so long?

How should you use the problems presented in this book? Set aside several 30- to 50-minute periods a week,—more if you have the time—during which you give students a number of problems from one chapter to explore. Or occasionally choose just one problem to explore in depth, allowing students to discuss and present different solutions to their classmates. This is a time to push the desks aside, use the gymnasium area, or go outdoors in order to have more space in which to move freely.

Besides these scheduled movement periods, arrange intermittent shorter time periods during which students solve one or more problems that pertain particularly to a concept you are teaching at that moment. For example, you may be introducing subtraction to your class. Either use a subtraction movement problem to introduce the concept, or after some initial discussion and verbal or written practice, give the students a subtraction movement problem that will reinforce the concept. Choose a simple one that they can solve standing right near their desks so you will not have to take the time to move furniture around. By using both long and short movement periods, you will be reinforcing academic concepts at the moment they are first introduced while also providing review periods several times weekly.

The movement problems in each chapter are listed in order of complexity and are adaptable to all grade levels (K-6) except where indicated. Many of the chapters provide movement experiences appropriate for preschool children. In general, specific grade levels are not indicated because I feel that this will allow you to be

9

more selective according to your classroom needs. You know far better than anyone how mature or imaginative your students are. Each class has its own individuality as does each student. To say that one activity should be confined only to the second grade level would be misleading.

During the presentation of the problems the basic elements of movement are introduced. The four elements of movement are *space, time, force,* and *flow.* The instrument or tool used to explore with is the *body.* With the body one *moves.* This sentence will help the students remember the elements of movement: My *body moves* in *space* and in *time* with *force* and with *flow.* Below is a list of the elements and dimensions of movement used in this book:

Body

Body parts:

head	spine	wrists	feet
neck	hips	fingers	heels
shoulders	arms	thumbs	ankles
chest	lower arms	legs	toes
waist	upper arms	thighs	
stomach	elbows	shins	
back	hands	knees	

Body surfaces:

front
back
sides

Body shapes (shapes the body can make):

curved
twisted
angular
narrow
wide
straight

Movement

Locomotor: movement through space from one point to another.

walk	skip
run	gallop
jump	slide
hop	crawl
leap	roll

Nonlocomotor: movement around the body's axis. Nonlocomotor movement does not take one through space. It is also known as *axial* or *stabilizing* movement.

bend	dodge	push-pull
twist	strike	rock-sway
stretch	fall	lift
swing	sit	shake

Space

Self space: space immediately around the body. Space used when doing nonlocomotor movement.

General space: space throughout the room. Space used when doing locomotor movement.

Direction: forward, backward, sideways (right and left), up and down; one moves through space in these directions.

Level: high, medium, low; the body or body parts can be on these levels in space.

Range: big, little, near to, far from; the relationship of body parts to each other or to other bodies.

Pathways: curved, straight, zigzag; one moves through space making pathways on the floor or in the air.

Focus: direction of gaze.

Time

Tempo: fast, medium, slow; the speed of movement (or music).

Pulse: an even measurement of time regardless of tempo.

Accent: a movement more forceful than the movements preceding or following it; just as in music where additional emphasis may be placed on certain pulse beats in a series.

Rhythmic patterns: a succession of movements or sounds of varying duration. An example of a rhythmic pattern: ♩♩ ♫

Force or Energy

Degrees: strong, medium, weak. The harder the muscles contract, the more body parts used, and the greater the range of movements, the stronger will be the force exerted. The opposite of these actions will create weak force.

Qualities: sustained—smooth, continuous flow of energy
percussive—quick, explosive release of energy
swinging—pendular movement with acceleration and deceleration of energy
vibratory—shaking, staccato movement with energy constantly starting and stopping

Flow

Free: ongoing, continuous, fluid movement

Bound: restrained, controlled, balanced movement

Use these terms often, encouraging the children to try their solutions on different levels, in different directions, with varying degrees of force. Of course, many of the terms will have to be explained and discussed when you introduce them. The more you use the terms and encourage the children to put them into practice, the greater their movement vocabulary will become. The result ultimately will be more varied and creative solutions to the problems.

The more elements you add to a problem, the more complex that problem becomes to solve. Therefore, use each of the elements individually before using them together. For example: the first day you may ask your students to make the letter *A* on a low level; next you might ask then to try moving their letter *A*'s in a backwards direction; a third challenge would be moving their

letter *A*'s in a curved pathway. When your students can successfully solve these problems, you can combine all three questions
into one: "Can you make the letter *A* on a low level, moving
backwards in a curved pathway?" This is quite a challenge!

I recommend using the problems in "The Alphabet," "Numbers,"
"Counting," and "The Body" to introduce the movement experiences at *every* grade level. These movement problems are simple
and fun, and for this reason, I recommend them as a good
introduction to this new movement experience. Moreover, many
of the other movement problems require the use of letter and
number shapes for their solutions. Practice in making letters and
numbers with the body is provided in the problems regarding the
alphabet, numbers, and counting. General body awareness is
developed in the problems regarding the body.

When you are ready to present a movement problem, choose one
that corresponds with the concept you are studying in class.
Present the problem to your students. If there is confusion,
rephrase the problem or return to a simpler one. Allow time for
your students to solve the problem. During this time reinforce and
help individuals that are having difficulties. If your students are
working on the first type of problem previously described—a
problem that has only one known acceptable solution— acknowledge those with the acceptable solution, and make sure that those
who did not solve the problem understand the solution.

If the students are working on the second or third type of
problems, acknowledge their efforts and then ask them to consider
other solutions. You might divide the class in half to have them
observe each other, or you might ask volunteers to demonstrate
their solutions to their classmates. Be sure to pick different
students each time so that you neither neglect nor overuse any
individuals. If time permits, discuss with students: the variety of
solutions; how the solutions differed; what different elements of
movement various individuals used in their solutions; how some
solutions were easier to do than others; why some solutions solved
the problem better than others; and any other problems that
might relate to the concept you are studying. When you feel the
problem is sufficiently explored and discussed, proceed to another
problem or subject. Always feel free to go back to the problem to
review or reinforce the concept you are working on.

There are some problems your students will want to do over and over again all year long. There are others that you might do a few times over a short period of time and then not again for several weeks. You must be careful to strike a happy medium with the problems you give your students. They must be challenging but not so difficult as to become discouraging. If you find the children are having trouble with a problem, go back to a simpler one and work up to the more complex one gradually. You have to be willing to experiment as you will find trial-and-error one of the most useful methods in presenting movement experiences.

A teacher is not a critic of movement experiences but a catalyst for them. The teacher is there to spark the children's imagination, not to judge their solutions. Reinforcement can be very important. It is critical that the children understand early that there is no failure in movement experiences. This will help them to release their inhibitions. By positively and frequently reinforcing all the children you will gain their confidence. Never force a child to participate. No one can be made to move against his or her will. Often you can solve classroom behavioral difficulties by ignoring the problem child's antics and by positively reinforcing the child who is engaged in the desired behavior. If left alone, the problem child will soon see how much fun classmates are having and will join in the fun.

Anything that is creative and exciting is often, but not invariably, accompanied by noise. The movement experiences in this book are often accompanied by silence because the children are answering questions through movement rather than orally. However, when the problems are solved through group exploration rather than individual exploration, there is usually what I call "working" noise. When children work together to solve a movement problem, some discussion is necessary. This is called "working" noise because it is productive. A classroom that is constantly quiet except for the sound of the teacher's voice is a place where a limited amount of learning is taking place.

However, there will be times when you want to interrupt the working noise in order to start a discussion or move on to a new problem. It is important to have some sort of signal which means "stop and listen." Your own voice is the least effective because it is the most often heard. Yelling above the activity only causes the noise level to increase. I prefer to use a small hand drum or two rhythm sticks made from a broom handle. This creates a very special and distinctive sound that immediately catches the children's attention. Two beats of my drum mean stop and listen. One drum beat means to begin solving the problem just given. I find this method to be extremely effective. I introduce the signal to the class in the form of a game called "Freeze." The children are given several very simple movement problems such as: move your arm all around you, see how many different places in space you can put your foot, etc. On two drum beats the children have to freeze and hold their positions until given one drum beat, the signal to move. With constant reinforcement for the good "freezers," the signals are learned quickly by all.

It is a common mistake to beat the drum and immediately start talking. Be sure to wait until you have everyone's attention before you continue with directions. Other signals you might use are hand clapping, finger snapping, finger cymbals, a tambourine, or a raised hand. These are acceptable but I have not found them to be as effective as a beat on the drum or sticks.

You may find that a special signal is not always necessary when working in the classroom. If you are presenting one or two simple movement problems that require little movement through general space, your regular classroom signal will probably be sufficient for maintaining control. You will find a special signal most helpful when working in a large, open area on problems that require much locomotor movement for their solutions.

Your voice is very important when presenting movement problems. A dramatic voice can be very helpful in motivating the children, especially in the primary grades. For example, if you are working with levels in space, speak in a high voice for high levels and a low voice for low levels. Let your voice show your interest and excitement with what the children are doing. You probably will not have trouble being heard in the classroom, but if you go outdoors, remember to speak loudly and clearly. Oftentimes children are concentrating so hard on their solutions and are so involved that they do not always hear your further directions. This is when the drum signal can be helpful.

When working for 30- to 50-minute periods, it is preferable to let the children take off their shoes and socks for the movement experiences. If the floor is not too cold or too rough, there is no reason why they should not be allowed to work barefoot. Not only is this a novel, and therefore stimulating experience, but it also helps children to be freer in their movements. This is not practical, however, when only presenting one or two short experiences in the classroom.

When working in a large empty area, I find that a circle formation is an excellent starting point. A circle is a very friendly arrangement because all the children can see each other. Often during the lesson I call the children back to the circle to open a discussion, to introduce a new problem, or simply to let them rest or calm down.

One of the most frequent questions I hear from teachers wanting to present movement experiences to their students is: how do you maintain class control when the children are moving around the room? First of all, much of the movement can be done in the students' self spaces near their desks. They do not have to move all around the classroom. When the activities do take the children through general space, there usually are few problems. If you have good control of your class already, including movement experiences in the curriculum can only make your control better by adding more enthusiasm and exercise. The movement problems are well structured and class control comes from this order. The structuring allows for freedom but not license. If you do not have good class control, the values of movement experiences may help change some of the negative conditions that have arisen in the classroom.

When presenting the movement problems be enthusiastic and confident. Be honest but positive in your feelings regarding the children's solutions and respect their feelings. If things seem to be going badly, reevaluate your own methods before turning to the children for the reason. It is my philosophy that the faults we see in children are usually reflections of bad examples set knowingly or not by some adults. There are many helpful ideas in the books on class management listed in the bibliography. Above all else, to create a positive and open atmosphere where movement experiences will thrive best, *you* must be open to change and be positive in your feelings about this new method of teaching.

When and Where

When should children be introduced to movement experiences? Movement experiences should be introduced into the elementary school curriculum at every grade level. Many of the experiences can be presented before elementary school. The activities are enjoyed by fifth-graders and preschoolers alike. However, you can expect different physical and social development at each level, and the movement problems should be presented with these differences in mind.

Three- to eight-year-olds do not work well in groups. They are still too ego-centered to have much group spirit or interaction. For this age range provide movement experiences that are individual in nature. Over half of the problems in each chapter are directed toward individual, rather than group, problem-solving. By the age of six, children begin to work well in partners, and toward the latter part of third grade, small group work can be introduced. Large group work can be introduced in the fourth grade and continued through the sixth grade. If you have a second grade class that seems ready to handle small group work, by all means introduce this type of experience. Characteristics of each age group overlap so you will have to be sensitive to the maturity of your children and proceed accordingly.

Children between the ages of three and eight are very inventive. They have good imaginations and are very curious. They love movement and will continually surprise you with their movement solutions. However, they have short attention spans so it is wise to vary the activity often.

17

Children in this age group are also very active and do well with gross motor skills. By the age of six, most children can skip. By the end of second grade, children should be able to walk and run in different directions, with their bodies on different levels, with changes in range, body shape, force and tempo, alone or with a partner. They should be able to jump, hop, leap, gallop, slide, and skip with changes in direction, range, force, and tempo. By the end of third grade, children should be able to perform all the locomotor and nonlocomotor movements with all the variations in space, time, force, and flow.

Nine- to twelve-year-olds go through a rapid growth period that seems to make them more inhibited about their bodies. Sex differences are more pronounced and this increases their inhibitions. They are very sensitive to criticism, so it is important to avoid making judgmental statements about their work. Always stress the positive aspects of their movement solutions.

Although children in this age group fully enjoy the movement experiences, they are more reticent in the beginning than the younger children. Therefore, it is more important to start with experiences that allow children to work in groups. They feel more confident at first when working with others. Start with movement experiences related to math, science, or spelling. Children of this age adore body spelling or making their own machines or math equations. After they have become freer in their movements, you may introduce lessons in some of the more complex areas such as emotions. At this time you may also include individual activities.

Nine- to twelve-year-olds should be able to explore in depth all the elements of movement intellectually as well as physically. Always challenge these children to add variety to their movements by combining the dimensions of space, time, force, and flow. They enjoy solving complex movement problems and inventing their own problems to present to classmates.

Discussion is an important part of movement experiences in the fourth, fifth, and sixth grades. The various aspects of their movement solutions should be discussed. The use of space, time, force, and flow, the academic concepts involved, body mechanics, locomotor and nonlocomotor movements are examples of good topics for discussion. Most important at this age, however, are elaborations by the children of their feelings regarding what they have done and seen. Nine- to twelve-year-olds are going through so many changes that cause confusion and bewilderment. They need a chance to discuss these feelings. Movement experiences provide the perfect setting.

Where are you going to find space for movement experiences? The answer is not as hard as you might think. As mentioned earlier, some of the problems can be solved with children sitting at their desks. Most can be solved standing near their desks or in front of the room. If you set aside a 30- to 50-minute period for movement experiences, you will have time to push the desks aside to form a large space in the center of the classroom. This is not only good exercise in itself but also sets the mood for this special activity. If well organized, the moving of desks will take only a few minutes. The children will soon learn that the faster they accomplish this task, the sooner they will be able to begin moving.

Be sure that your classroom is a safe place to move in. Check to see if anything can fall down or be shaken loose by the extra activity in the room. Also, be sure the floor is free of tacks and other debris. You should set up some safety rules for the children. Examples include: avoid the furniture and walls, keep all objects out of the mouth while moving, avoid bumping or pushing each other, only shoes or bare feet allowed (socks are very slippery and dangerous), etc. These rules should be clearly defined before beginning. It is nice to have the children help make up the rules for their movement area. They seem to follow them better when they have had a hand in their formulation.

If you have access to a multipurpose or gymnasium area, you can conduct class there. However, these areas are often available only for scheduled physical education classes. Of course, if you are the gym teacher this problem is solved. An empty stage is a nice area in which to work. A grassy playground is another perfect area in which to move, especially if good weather prevails. A cement playground is satisfactory if there is no other space available, but it can be quite hard on the shins and knees when jumping, hopping, or leaping. And it will not be very pleasant to crawl or roll on. However, there are many activities that do not involve these actions and are adaptable to a cement surface.

You may decide to always use the same area to work in or at various times you may use all the areas I have described. In either case you will be giving students the freedom of movement.

Designing Your Own

There may be content areas included in your curriculum that are not covered in this book. It is my hope that, after using this book for several months, you will be familiar enough with the material to be able to design your own movement experiences for those subjects. The children will also delight in being asked to design experiences for each other.

When designing new movement experiences, there are several factors to bear in mind that will make the experiences most meaningful:

1. Ensure success for each student. De-emphasize competitive games.

2. Try to involve all the children all of the time. Avoid long lines of children waiting for turns.

3. Encourage children to explore the variety of solutions available through the use of the elements of movement.

4. Be clear and specific in your directions.

5. Be positively reinforcing.

As for the problems that are in the book, I encourage you to rephrase them in your own language so that you feel comfortable presenting them. You may expand or shorten individual problems to fit your schedule. You will find the elements of movement can be used to add new perspectives to old problems.

When designing your own problems, or using the ones in this book, it is helpful when aiming for varied and creative movement to be quite specific in your use of movement terminology. Instead of using the general terms *space, time, force,* and *flow* in your directions as has sometimes appeared in the text, ask the students to try moving backwards and sideways, at high and low levels, with large and small movements, slowly and quickly, with tight and loose muscles, etc. This guidance is particularly useful early in your students' movement experiences, providing a solid foundation for later, richer experiences.

Above all, try to allow the methods put forth in this book to serve as a vehicle for the boundless creative energies of children discovering the uniqueness of their own minds and bodies. The rewards will be great for student and teacher alike.

PART I

LANGUAGE ARTS PROBLEMS

Poems

Spelling

Comparatives

Rhyming

Stories

Reading Alphabet

The Alphabet

1. Can you turn your whole body into a letter of the alphabet we have been working on today? What about a *C*? *(Start with easy letters such as* T, C, I, F, J, O, U, V, Y.*)*

2. Can you make the first letter of your first name? Can you make the first letter of your last name?

3. Can you make an *A* with your hands? with your arms? with just your legs? with a leg and an arm? *(Continue with other body parts and other letters.)*

4. What letters can you make with a partner? *(Have the students watch each other and guess the letters.)*

5. What letters can you make with three people? Are some letters easier to make with three people than with just one person? [*W, M, A, G, H, K, R, Q, N*] Why? [These letters use more lines and angles than others.]

6. Can you make an *A* standing up? sitting down? lying down? *(Here children are using different* levels.*)*

7. Can you make a capital *A*? Can you make a small *a*? *(Here children are using* range.*)*

8. Who can show me all the vowels?

9. Can your letter skip across the room and still keep its shape?

Can you make a letter of the alphabet lying down? These children found the floor was perfect for making the letter *K*. ("The Alphabet," Problem 6)

Who can show me a hopping *T*? a rolling *O*? a running *I*? a jumping *P*? a galloping *Y*? a walking *B*?

Continue to combine different locomotor movements with different letters. Ask the children to come up with challenges for each other. You might want to save this activity for gym or recess when you are in a space with more room than the classroom.

10. Can you make a frozen *Z*? When I give the signal melt into another letter, freeze, and let us guess what your new letter is. *(You may want to ask them to melt into another specific letter. This problem uses free and bound flow.)*

11. Make the largest *T* you can, a *T* an elephant would write. Now make the smallest *T* you can— a *T* for an ant. *(Here range is used.)*

Can your letter P *gallop through space?* ("The Alphabet," Problem 9)

12. Can your letter walk backwards, forwards, sideways? *(Use of direction.)*

13. I'm going to turn your elbow into a pencil. How can you write the letter *A* in the air with your elbow? Can you write the letter *A* with your head? with your knee? with your leg? with your shoulder? Trace the letter on the ceiling, on the floor, in front of you, behind you. *(Continue, using other letters and other body parts.)*

14. Let us make "kite" letters. Turn your body into the shape of your favorite letter *(or you may choose to give a letter)*. Now let the wind catch your kite letter and fly through the air. The wind becomes stronger and stronger, you are blowing all around. Remember to keep the shape of your letter. Now the wind is dying down and you are falling slowly back to the ground until you land gently on the grass. Are you still in the shape of your letter? *(Use of force.)*

This is a marvelous activity for a windy recess period or when the children are restless or excited. You can also use the idea with "balloon" letters. The balloon has a leak and falls gently to the ground.

15. Who can show me the letter that begins the word *cat? (Use harder words and initial blends for older children.)* Remember to make the letter with your body, not your mouth. Somebody else give a word for us to solve.

16. Find a friend and trace a letter on your friend's back. Can your friend guess what letter you traced? Now let your friend trace a letter on your back.

17. Find a partner. One of you is a pencil and one is a writer. The writer is going to stand behind the pencil with his or her hands on the pencil's shoulders. Now guide your pencil slowly in the shape of a big letter. Your pencil's feet will write the letter on the floor as you move him or her around. Can your pencil

One of you is a writer and the other is a pencil. Here the writers are guiding their pencils in the shapes of letters. Can the pencil guess what letter was written? ("The Alphabet," Problem 17)

guess what letter you wrote? If not, try again. Remember to go slowly so your pencil has time to think. *(A good activity for developing kinesthetic awareness and sensory-motor perception.)*

18. I'm going to give you a word. Make the first letter of the word with your body; then when I give the signal become the word. For example, I might say "DOG." You would make the letter *D* then you would make the shape and actions of a dog. If I said "HAPPY," could you make the letter *H* with your body and then show me how a happy person would look and act?

If you are able to find The Marcel Marceau Alphabet Book *by George Mendoza, it will be helpful in giving you and your students ideas for this activity. Encourage their own interpretations besides copying the actions in the book. Each child might make an alphabet book like Marceau's thinking of a word and drawing his or her body in the shape of that word.*

19. Let us go through the alphabet and see if we can find a body part to match each letter. Then try to make the shape of the letter with that body part. For example, *A*—arm; make the letter *A* as best you can with your arm. Can you think of another body part that begins with the letter *A*? That's right—ankle. Can you use your ankle and another body part to make the letter *A*?

Not all the letters will match with a body part. The children can think of a word other than a body part to use for these letters.

20. Can you sing the alphabet song and make each letter as you sing it? How fast can you sing the song and still form all the letters? Have a contest with a friend.

21. How many different ways can you make the letter *A* with your body or body parts? *(Continue, using other letters.)* What letter in the alphabet had the greatest variety of solutions? *(This could be a continuous contest.)*

22. Let us play the "Grandmother's Suitcase" game. Going through the alphabet, first name the object grandmother put

in her suitcase, and then make the shape of the letter and the shape of the object with your body. Each new person must remember and become the previous objects listed. For example, the first person might say: Grandmother put an apple in her suitcase. That person would then make the letter *A* and the shape of an apple. The second person would say: Grandmother put an apple and a ball in her suitcase. He or she would make an *A*, an apple shape, a *B*, and a ball shape. The third person would continue with *A* and *B* and add *C*. You will be surprised at how much easier it is to remember the list when you make the letter and object with your body rather than just saying it.

23. Can you make up your own alphabet? Make up some crazy letters and show us their shapes. Can you give your letters a name? Can you do all the things with these crazy letters that you did with the regular alphabet letters?

    (You might have the older children get in groups to make crazy letters to show to the other groups. The Dr. Seuss book On Beyond Zebra *is delightful to read before presenting this problem.)*

Reading Readiness

In addition to these problems, the following problems in "Math Readiness" may be used for reading readiness: Problems 1 and 2, 5 and 6, 7 and 8, and 15 and 16.

1. Find a partner to work with. One of you make a high shape, a shape that stretches to the ceiling. The other person make a low shape, a shape that is near the floor. Freeze in your shapes. Good. Now the low shape become a high shape, and the high shape make a low shape.

   With very young children you may have to tell each child which shape to be. They often have trouble deciding this matter between themselves. Variation: Have each pair perform one at a time. Let the other children name the child who is low and the child who is high.

2. I am going to hold up a card with a lower-case letter on it. Look carefully at the letter; then make the shape of the same letter in the upper case. I am holding up an *e*. Can you show me a upper-case *E* by using your body parts to form the letter? Let's try another letter.

3. Turn your head so that you are looking over your left shoulder. Now slowly move your head until you are looking over your right shoulder. Snap your head around to the left. As you move your head slowly to the right again, use your eyes and look at all the things in the room that are around

you. *(Repeat this exercise several times varying the speed that the head moves to the right.)*

Can you draw a line on the floor with your right leg moving from left to right? Now try with your left leg. Can you stretch your arms to the left and reach out in space as you move them to the right? Show me how you can punch holes in space moving your fists from left to right. *(Continue with other body actions which move from left to right.)*

4. I am going to draw four pictures on the board. One of the pictures does not belong with the other ones. Can you show me which picture does not belong by making the shape of the odd picture with your body?

You might draw three circles and one square, three S's and a Z, three squares and a triangle, etc. (See Diagram 1.) When the children master these problems, use foursomes such as: three articles of clothing and a tree, three kinds of flowers and a toy, three types of food and a spoon, etc.

Diagram 1. ("Reading Readiness," Problem 4)

Diagram 2. ("Reading Readiness," Problem 5)

5. *On the chalkboard, draw a series of four noses or animal heads all pointing in the same direction except one that points in the opposite direction. (see Diagram 2.)*

   Look at the four noses I have drawn on the board. Which one is pointing in a different direction from the others? Can you show me by pointing your arm in the direction the odd nose is pointing? Good. Look at the next four noses. Point your leg in the direction the odd nose is pointing. *(Continue with other foursomes and different body parts pointing such as elbow, head, and knee.)*

6. I am going to write two words on the board. *(Use pairs that are often reversed such as* tip *and* pit, pot *and* top, tap *and* pat, bat *and* tab, but *and* tub, *etc.)* I will point to one of the words. Can you show me that you know the meaning of the word by describing the word through movement? *(Point to words that are more easily described such as* pat, tip, bat, *etc.)*

Variation: Number the words in the pair (1 and 2). Draw or hold up a picture of one of the words. Ask the children to show you the number of the word that is illustrated by making the shape of the number or by touching the number of body parts to the floor.

7. I am going to draw a shape on the board. Can you make the same shape with your body? *(Use geometric shapes, letter shapes, and number shapes.)*

8. Who would like to come to the front of the room to make a shape for the rest of the class to copy? When you have your shape, freeze so that the rest of us can study it carefully and copy the shape exactly. *(This exercise provides good practice in visual discrimination.)*

9. Everyone who is wearing the color red make a curved shape. Is everyone who is curved wearing red? Are there any people wearing red who are not curved? Now "reds" sit down. Everyone wearing green jump up and down. Everyone wearing

Can you copy the shape exactly? ("Reading Readiness," Problem 8)

blue make a strong, muscular shape. Everyone wearing white move their arms very quickly. Everyone wearing brown make a big shape. Everyone wearing orange make a tiny shape.

Continue in this fashion with other colors and other elements of movement. If any child in your class is color blind you may not want to do this activity.

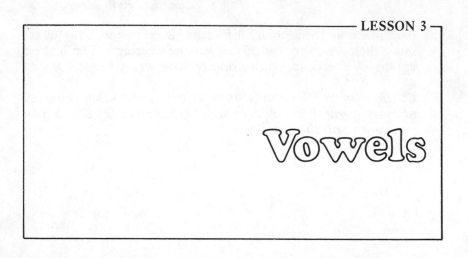

Vowels

In Problems 1-4, long vowel words may be substituted for short vowel words or long and short vowel words may be used together.

1. Can you make the letter *a* with your body? Listen to the *a* sound in the word *as*. That is the short *a* sound. Say that sound as you move your letter *a* through space; in a circle; to another level.

   (Continue with o, on; i, it; u, us; *and* e, egg.*)*

2. I am going to say a word with a short vowel sound. Repeat the word. Can you make the shape of the vowel sound you hear in the word?

   You will be able to easily spot children who are having difficulty hearing the correct vowel sound. Continue with other words.

3. I am going to hold up a picture of an object that has a short vowel sound. Can you make an object with your body that has a similar vowel sound? We will try to guess each other's words.

   Example: You hold up a picture of a sled. The children can make the shape of a bed, head, bell, pen, etc.

4. *(This activity can be done in reading groups, when written*

work is finished, or during free time.) Find a partner. One of you make the shape of an object whose name has a short vowel sound. The other partner now guesses what the object is, says the name of the object, and makes a different object with the same vowel sound. Keep alternating words until you run out of ideas for that vowel sound. Then go to another vowel sound. *(Example: One child makes the shape of a hat. The partner would say "hat" and then make the shape of a cat.)*

5. Can you make a high level shape when you hear me say a short vowel sound and a low level shape when you hear a long vowel sound? *(Go through a list of different words. Do not always alternate long and short.)* This time try bending on the short vowels and stretching on the long vowels; move forward on long, backward on short; quickly on short, slowly on long; sharply on short, smoothly on long; move your arm on long sounds, your leg on short sounds.

Go through one list with the same set of movements. The next day try a new challenge. This game may be varied by holding up pictures instead of saying words.

6. When we put a silent *e* on the end of a word, the vowel sound changes from short to long. Who would like to come up and spell out the word *cut*? We need three people. Make small short letters because this is a short-vowel-sound word. Who would like to be the silent *e*? Come up and add yourself to the word. What new word did we make? All the letters should change shape to long, big letters because now we have a long-vowel-sound word. Let's try another word. Can someone give me a new short-vowel-sound word that we could add a silent *e* to? *(Continue reminding the children to change the shape of their letters when the silent e is added.)*

7. Who can spell out a word that has a silent *e*? We need at least four people. Everyone say out loud the word you see. Now I am going to ask the silent *e* to sit down. Now say the word you see. Can the letters change shape as the word changes? Can the people at their desks become frozen statues that express the word they see? Change your statue as you see the word change its meaning.

What happens when you add a silent e *to the word sit?* The vowel *i* changes from short to long. The students are describing this change by making the letters in the long-vowel-sound word — site — longer and larger than the letters in the short-vowel-sound word. ("Vowels," Problem 6)

Some good words to use are: hate-hat, tube-tub, pale-pal, note-not, hope-hop, tape-tap, pine-pin, cube-cub, wine-win.

8. I am going to write two consonants on the board with a space between them. Can you think of a vowel to put between the two consonants that would spell a word? If you can, make the shape of the vowel with your body. Let's look at the vowels you are making and write them down on the board. How many different words did we make with these two consonants? Can you think of any more? Let's try two more consonants. *(Use pairs such as: m__n, p__n, p__t, t__p, b__d, etc.)*

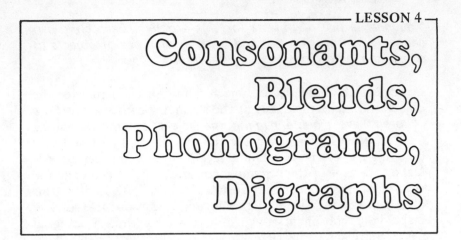

Consonants, Blends, Phonograms, Digraphs

In Problems 1 and 2 and 4-7, a blend or digraph can be substituted for a single consonant. If Problems 1 and 4 are used for blends or digraphs, the children should work in pairs. Phonograms can be substituted for single consonants in Problems 1, 2, 5, and 7.

1. I am going to hold up a picture. Name the picture in your head. Now can you make the shape of the beginning consonant with your body? Can you make the shape of the ending consonant?

   It will be easy for you to see the children who are having trouble. If you are working on end sounds be sure to pick pictures that end in consonants.

2. I'm going to put a picture on the bulletin board *(or chalk tray)*. Now I will hold up, one at a time, consonant cards. When you see me hold up the beginning consonant of the picture, stand up as quickly as possible. When I hold up the ending consonant, sit down.

   For the picture of a dog you might hold up t, b, p, k, d, f, s, g, r, l. Omit ending consonants if the children are not ready. Try other actions such a push, pull, twist, turn, punch, stroke, stamp, clap, swing, shake, etc.

3. *Problem 22 in "The Alphabet" is an excellent activity for initial sounds.*

4. *You need a bag of objects for this problem. Each child can choose a consonant letter and bring a small bag of objects to school that all begin with his or her letter.*

I am going to hold up an object. Think of the name for the object and make the shape of the beginning consonant. *(If the children have trouble naming the object, say the name out loud together.)* Can you make the consonant on a low level? on a high level? or a medium level? Here is another object. Make the shape of the beginning consonant. Can you make the consonant move backward? forward? right? left? Look at this object. Make the shape of the beginning consonant. Can you make your consonant move in a curved pathway? a zigzag path? a straight path? Here is another object. Make the shape of its beginning consonant. Show me a giant consonant; a tiny consonant; a medium-sized consonant. With what letter does this object begin? Make its shape. Can you show me a strong, muscular consonant? a weak, loose consonant? Here is one more object; make the shape of its beginning consonant. Show me how quickly your consonant can move just in your self space, perhaps while changing levels or turning around. How slowly can your consonant move?

This problem provides an excellent review of all the elements of movement while working on initial sounds. Ending sounds may also be practiced. Pictures may be used instead of objects but the bringing of objects serves an extra purpose in that children are working on initial sounds at home while finding their objects to bring to school.

5. Find a partner. Draw a consonant on your partner's back or move your partner around the floor to walk out the shape of a consonant. Your partner has to guess the consonant. Then your partner should name and act out all the words he or she can think of that begin with that consonant. Can you think of any other words that your partner did not think of? You act them out. Now let your partner draw a consonant on your back.

6. Find a partner. One of you make the shape of a toy or plaything (ball, top, house, bunny, jacks, jump rope, etc.). The other partner thinks of what letter the toy begins with and

makes the shape of the letter with body parts or his or her whole body. Did you guess the toy correctly? Did you get the beginning consonant right? Change leaders and try another toy. Keep going until you run out of ideas. *(Other categories you might use: food, animals, actions, emotions.)*

7. Let's divide into groups. Each group will think of a consonant *(or you may assign different consonants).* Each member of the group make a different object that begins with your group's consonant. You may work together if you wish. *(If you are in a large area ask the object to move in and through space.)* When you are ready, we will try to guess your group's consonant by guessing the objects we see. *(This problem may be done with ending consonants also.)*

8. Let us divide into two groups. The people in the first group find partners. With your partner make two consonants that form a blend such as *pl, tr,* etc. When the first group is ready,

Can you describe through movement a word that begins with the blend tr-? The girl on the right is describing a tree as she stands next to the children acting out the blend. ("Consonants, Blends, Phonograms, Digraphs," Problem 8)

the people in the second group will find a blend for which they can think of a word. Then they will act out the word next to the blend. Now let's go around and guess the words.

9. *(Divide the students into 3 or 4 groups.)* I am going to give each group a card with a word ending (phonogram) written on it. *(You might use* ake, ay, ack, ight, ink, ank, ing, ang.*)* In your group try to think of as many words as possible by adding a consonant, consonant blend, or digraph to your ending. When it is your group's turn, I will hold up the ending, and your group will come up and form with your bodies the consonants, blends, and digraphs you thought of.

(After each group has finished, continue.) Can anyone think of any words the group missed?

Let each consonant, blend, or digraph stand beside the ending so that the other children can see the words clearly. This activity may also be done without groups, having the whole class looking at one ending at a time and asking for individual responses.

10. *(Divide the class into two groups, one larger than the other.)* Can the people in the large group get together with as many friends as they need to spell out a phonogram (word ending) of their choice? Let us see how many different phonograms the large group can spell out. *(You may want to write a list of phonograms on the board such as* ay, ake, ing, ight, air, ail, oy etc.*)*

The people in the smaller group are going to be consonants. Make the shape of a consonant you like. Then find a phonogram to which you can add your consonant shape to make a word. Make your shape in front of the ending to spell a word. Let us try to use all the endings.

Can you stay in your shape and look around at the other words to see what new words we made? Can each consonant stay with its ending and make a new consonant to form a new word? Can each phonogram change to form a new word with its consonant? Can each consonant stay in its shape and move to a new phonogram? Can each phonogram stay together in its shape and find a new consonant? *(Encourage the children to move with changes in levels, directions, range, force, speed.)*

11. *Use consonant blends and digraphs in place of consonants in Problem 10. Be sure you think of phonograms that work well with blends such as* ink, ank, ay, ake, ight, ack.

12. I am going to write a word on the board, but I am going to leave off the initial consonant *(or blend). (Some examples are* -ap, -ed.*)* Can you think of a consonant to put in front of these letters that will form a word? When you think of one, make the shape of the consonant with your body. Let's look at the different consonants people are making and write them on the board. What new words have we made? *(This activity may also be done using ending consonants and examples such as* ta-, ma-.*)*

Rhyming

1. Who would like to come to the front of the room and spell out with their bodies the word *ball*? We need at least four people. *(When the word is spelled out, continue.)* How could we change the first letter to make another word? That's a good idea. Come up here to make the new letter, and *b* stand aside. Who can change the word again? *(Continue until all possibilities have been tried. Keep the other letters in front of the room so the students can see them and remember the other words.)* Now let us try the word *tell. (Continue this activity with other rhyming words.)*

2. I'm going to write a word on the board. *(Example:* ill.*)* Show me all the different letters you could use at the beginning of the word to change the meaning of it. Can you make the letters with different body parts or your whole body? As you make each letter, you might want to write the letters or words down so you will remember them. Who found the most letters? Read your list for us. Did anyone else make any other letters? Are those all real words? Let us try another word.

3. Who can give me a word that rhymes with *night*? Can you show me through movement what the word means?

   If the word is light, *you might see someone turning on a light, being the sun, being a light bulb, or picking up a feather. Have many children demonstrate their solutions, and comment on the different examples.*

Can you think of a word that rhymes with fed? This child is demonstrating one solution — a bed. ("Rhyming," Problem 3)

Now, who can give me another word that rhymes with *night*? Show me what the word means.

In addition to reinforcing rhyming skills, this is an excellent activity for word recognition and creative problem solving. You may want to write the words on the chalkboard to reinforce spelling and recognition.

4. I'm going to show you a picture. Now I will say a list of words, and every time you hear a word that rhymes with the picture word, jump up. *(Example: Show a picture of a hat and say the words* tell, sat, big, ran, cat, be, bat. *The students should jump up on* sat, cat, *and* bat.*)*

This time, each time you hear a rhyming word, try an arm movement; a head movement; a leg movement; change level;

change direction. *(Try a new movement for each new picture word.)*

5. *(Divide the students into groups.)* I am going to write a two-line rhyme on the chalkboard. *(If the children are too young to read, say the rhyme orally.)* I will leave the last word in the second line blank. The first group to figure out the rhyming word and to spell it correctly with their bodies wins.

   The younger children can do a body action to describe the word if they are unable to spell it. Here are some examples of rhymes:

   I like to eat
   all my____

   I bounce the ball
   over the____

   The big bee
   stung____

   I was so cold on the boat
   I had to put on my____

   My head is too fat
   to put on my____

   I cannot tell
   what is that bad____

   My dog bit
   my catcher's____

6. Find a partner. Write a word on your partner's back that has words that rhyme with it. Your partner has to think of a rhyming word and write it on your back. Keep alternating rhyming words until you run out of ideas. Instead of writing on backs, try spelling the words out with your bodies; acting out the words; drawing the words in the air.

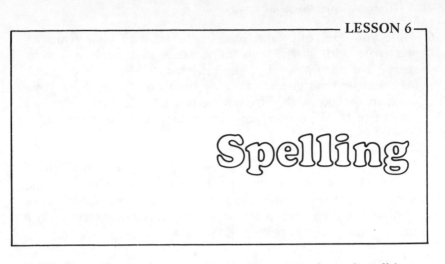

1. Pick one of your spelling words for the week, and spell it out using just your hands and fingers; now your arms; your legs; arms and legs; your whole body (or body parts).

2. Can you spell the word with your body standing up to make the letters? sitting or kneeling? lying on the floor? *(levels)*

3. Try spelling the word using general space. Draw the word on the ceiling with your finger; try your elbow on the wall; your knee on the floor; your head. Check your paper to be sure you are spelling the word correctly. *(pathways and levels)*

4. Someone give the class a spelling word and a body part. Pretend the body part is a giant pencil and write the word in the biggest letters our space will allow; now try the smallest letters. Let's try all the words, big and small.

Keep asking for words and body parts. To check their spelling, it is helpful to have the children spell out loud as they are writing their words in space. This exercise provides good exploration of range.

5. Can you spell out your word while jumping? Jump once as you say each letter. Can you hop? walk? run? skip? gallop? Now try jumping the shape of each letter on the floor. You may have to do a lot of jumps to draw each letter instead of doing one jump. Can you gallop to spell the word? run? walk? slide the shape of the letters?

6. While you spell out your word in the air with your arm, can you write with sharp, tense movements as though you were angry? Now try smooth, light movements. Now lie on your back and pretend you are floating on a quiet lake. Write your word in the sky with different body parts. Say each letter as you write it to be sure you are spelling the word correctly. *(Use of force.)*

7. Find a partner and write your spelling words on each other's backs. Have your partner say each letter as you write it and say the complete word when you are all done. Check your spelling list after each word to see if you were correct. If you made a mistake, try spelling the word again.

8. Can you write your spelling word in great big letters on a low level with your elbow? in small letters on a high level with your head? with sharp movements and big letters at a medium level with your knee?

Keep trying problems that involve range, levels, body parts and force at the same time. This is quite a challenge! After

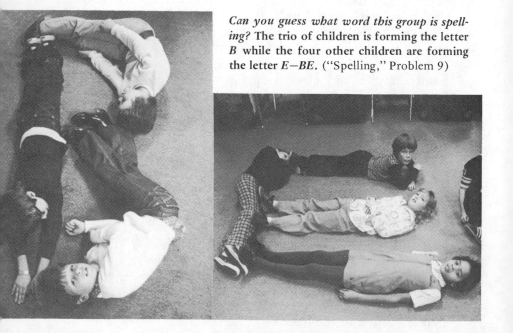

Can you guess what word this group is spelling? The trio of children is forming the letter *B* while the four other children are forming the letter *E—BE*. ("Spelling," Problem 9)

students have spelled a word with their bodies, go over the word with them verbally as they rewrite it in space. This repetition will encourage and reinforce the correct spelling.

Problems 9-13 work best with children ages 8-12 because they work well in groups.

9. I am going to divide you into groups. *(You might count off, use rows, girls against boys, etc. Be sure there are enough students in each group to spell the longest word.)* Each group will pick a word from the spelling list to spell as a group. Each person be a letter. If you have more people than letters, get together in twos and threes to form letters. When each group has figured out its word, I will ask a group to come up in front of the class and show the word.

   The people watching write the word down on your papers the way you think it is spelled correctly. Can you guess the first group's word? Did they spell it correctly? Did you spell it on your paper correctly? Let's try another group's word.

10. Let's get into groups. Pick a spelling word and write the word with each person making a letter in the word. Try to make all the letters on a high level; on a medium level; on a low level.

11. Form a spelling word with your group. Then try moving the whole word through space. Can you keep the shapes of your different letters and your word together as you move? Can you move your word forward? backward? sideways? Can you move your word quickly? slowly?

12. Form a spelling word with your group. Now scramble all the letters so that they are in the wrong order. Show your scrambled word to the rest of the class. They will try to guess the spelling word and write it correctly on their papers. Now who can move the letters around to spell the right word? Check your papers to see if you spelled the word correctly. Let's try another group.

13. After your group has formed a spelling word, act the word out. If your word is *train*, you might all join together to make a train and move around the room. If your word is *cat*, you

could each move the way you think a cat might move. If your word is *angry*, how could you move? Be sure to spell the word first. Let's try to guess what each group is spelling and doing. *(Some words are difficult to act out, like* to *or* become, *but children come up with very interesting solutions.)*

14. This time I'm going to give you a hard word that is not on your spelling list. Get together in your group and see if you can decide on the correct spelling. Put your word together and show the class. Can the rest of you guess the word? Did the group spell it correctly? *(Students enjoy this challenge.)*

Problems 15-23 require the use of equipment such as balls, beanbags, hoops, and wands—however, some of these problems may be easily adapted for classrooms without equipment.

15. We are going to play a game called "Dribble Spelling." I am going to give you a spelling word, and I want you to bounce or dribble the ball on the floor to spell out the word. Try big bounces and little bounces, big letters and little letters.

    (After you have given the student several words, go on.) Now pick a spelling word and first bounce out the number of letters in the word. If there are seven letters, there should be seven bounces. Then write the spelling word out while dribbling the ball, and we will try to guess your word.

    This problem can be done in groups also, with one ball for each group. As each student finishes a letter, he or she passes the ball to the next student.

16. Let's try playing "Toss Spelling." This games is just like "Dribble Spelling" except that we will toss the ball instead of dribbling it.

Problems 17-23 can be done at stations set up around the room. With this method, you need less equipment. Use a different piece of equipment at each station.

17. Say your spelling words out loud. While you spell them, bounce or toss your ball once for each letter. A friend can give you the words and check to see if you are spelling them

correctly. See if you can get through the whole list without missing a word, a bounce, or a toss.

18. As you jump rope, spell your words out loud. Jump for each letter. How quickly can you jump and spell? How many tricks can you do with your rope and spell at the same time? If you are jumping with a long rope, have the turners give you the word and check your spelling.

19. Try to balance a wand on the palm of your hand while you are spelling your words out loud. Can you balance for as long as it takes you to spell a word? Try to balance the wand on other body parts as you spell your words.

20. Find a partner and toss, roll, or slide a ball, a beanbag, a hoop, or a wand between you as you spell a word. Each of you will alternate tossing and giving the next letter in the word. If you miss the catch or misspell the word, start again.

Can you toss a beanbag in the air and spell a word before you catch it? ("Spelling," Problem 21)

21. Toss a beanbag in the air and see if you can spell a word before you catch it. Have a race with a friend. Be sure you are spelling the word correctly.

22. Roll a hoop along the floor, and spell your word out as you tap the hoop forward.

23. As you walk across the balance beam, say a letter for each step. Can you make the shape of each letter with your arms as you walk and spell and still keep your balance?

24. Let's play "Spelling Baseball." First we will divide into two teams. To get a single, the batter must spell correctly the word I pitch to him or her. If you misspell the word, that is an out. If you spell the word correctly, you get to try for a double. For a double, the batter must make each letter of the word with his or her body. If you make the double, then you can try for a triple. To get a triple, the batter must use the word correctly in a sentence. If you score a triple, then you have a chance for a home run. For a home run I will give you a very hard word to spell. You will have thirty seconds to meet with your team and try to spell the word correctly with your bodies.

We will use one corner of the room as home plate and the other three corners as bases. Someone should always be in the on-deck circle waiting for a turn at bat. Remember—three outs and the next team is up to bat.

25. *Make a letter grid on a large sheet of paper and tape it to the floor, or project a grid on the floor or wall.*

How many different words can you find on this grid? Spell out words by putting one body part on each letter until your word is formed.

Variation: (a) The squares used to spell the words must touch each other somehow. (b) Jump, hop, leap, skip from letter to letter to spell a word. (c) Play with a partner or group. Take turns touching body parts to letters to form one word as a group. The last person to touch a letter to form a word gets a point. Once a letter has been touched the body parts must stay on that square. The students playing the game will become twisted around as in the popular game of "Twister."

26. *Write a list of words with prefixes and suffixes on the chalkboard such as* dislike, unhappy, untie, gladly, burned, blowing, disobey, depart, inside, darkness.

   Look at the list of words on the board. Who can spell out with body shapes the prefix or suffix you see in one of the words? You may ask some friends to help you make the letters. *(Continue with the rest of the words.)*

27. *(Divide the students into groups of seven or eight.)* I am going to give each group a root word. Can you make two new words by adding a prefix or suffix? Spell out each new word one at a time with your group, and the rest of us will try to guess your root word.

   Some good root words to use for this problem are pack, like, kind, friend, slow, thank, call, long, ask, big, blow, kind, jump, dark, dear, deep, friend, happy.

Synonyms

1. Who can say a sentence that contains a word that has a synonym? When you come to the word, make a shape with your whole body and hold that shape. Who can think of a synonym for the word? Make the exact same shape as the first person and say your synonym. Can anyone think of another synonym? Make the same shape as the first two people and say your synonym.

   Continue until no more synonyms are suggested. This is an excellent exercise for shape recognition.

2. *(Write a list of words that have apparent synonyms on the board.)* When you think of a synonym for the word on the chalkboard, make a shape. Who can think of another synonym? This time make the exact same shape as the person with the first synonym, but then change one small part of the shape to be different. A synonym is a word that has a similar meaning to another word, but it is a differently shaped and spelled word. So make your shape similar but not exactly the same. Who can think of another synonym and a similar shape?

   Continue as before until all the synonyms are exhausted. Keep the shapes in front of the room so the students can see the similarity in design. Write each student's synonym on the chalkboard above his or her shape.

3. I'm going to write a word on the board. The first person to think of a synonym come to the front and make the first letter of your synonym with your body. Who can think of a synonym that begins with that letter? If you can think of another synonym, come up and make the first letter. Then we will try to guess the synonym you are thinking of.

4. Instead of making a shape for your synonym, try doing a very short movement pattern that describes your synonym. Who can think of another synonym and copy the first pattern? Let's do this in partners. The first person will say a word and do a movement. The second person will give a synonym and copy that movement. Now switch leaders. *(This is a good memory exercise.)*

Antonyms

5. I am going to write on the board *(or say out loud)* a pair of words that have the opposite meaning. Who can show through movement what the first word means? Who can show through movement what the second word means? Now, everybody try to describe the two words through movement. Did you do movements that were quite different?

Some excellent antonyms for movement are: large-small, high-low, loud-soft, fast-slow, tight-loose, sticky-fluffy, straight-curved, still-active, smooth-jerky, flat-sharp.

6. I am going to write on the board *(or say out loud)* a word. I want you to think of the opposite of the word and do movement that describes the word you're thinking of. I see many (low) movements. Your antonym must be (low). *(If you are in a classroom, write the antonym next to its opposite on the chalkboard.)*

7. Find a partner. One partner will do a movement. Can you do the opposite of what your partner did? Now, tell each other the words you were thinking of in your head. Were they antonyms? If your partner ran, did you walk? If your partner moved on a low level, did you move on a high level? If your partner made a wide movement, did you make a narrow one? Try another pair of antonyms. Let's watch some partners, and see if we can guess what two words they are doing.

Can you do the opposite of what your partner did? Here one partner is still and the other partner is active. ("Synonyms, Antonymns, Homonyms," Problem 7)

8. Let's form two straight lines facing each other. I am going to stand behind one line so they cannot see me but the other line can. I will hold up a word card, and the line that can see the word act out the antonym for the word. The line with their backs to me try to guess the word on my card by looking at the other line's movements and thinking of a word to describe the opposite of what you are seeing. Now, I will go behind the other line and have them act out a new word.

Some antonyms you might try are: hot-cold, fat-thin, old-young, pretty-ugly, rich-poor, sick-healthy, happy-sad, bored-interested, war-peace, calm-excited, weak-strong. *Ask the students for more antonyms.*

Homonyms

9. I am going to put a word on the board *(or hold up a word card)*. Who can think of a word that sounds the same but is spelled differently and has a different meaning? Can you act out both words? When you act out your word, remember to try different levels, directions, range, force and speed.

10. Find a partner. I'm going to give each of you a pair of homonyms. Act out your words, one at a time, and try to guess each other's word. Can you spell your partner's word correctly on his or her back? draw it in the air with different body parts? spell it with your body?

11. I'm going to divide the class into groups. I will give a word to one group, and they will spell it with their bodies. As soon as you have figured out what their word is, think of a homonym and spell it with your group. The first group to spell the homonym correctly will start the next word.

1. *(Distribute readers, index cards, and scissors to the students.)* Look in your reader and find a compound word. Write the word on the card in big letters. Now cut the word in half so that it becomes two words. I am going to collect all the cards in the room, mix them up, and pass one out to each of you. Move around the room with your card. When you find a person with a word that goes with your word, get together and act out the compound word. When everyone has a partner, we will look at the pairs and try to guess the word.

   Variation: play music as the children move around. When you stop the music, they must find the correct partner as quickly as possible and make the word. Have the children move in different ways as they look for their partners, e.g., skipping, galloping, sliding, crawling, etc.

2. I am going to put a list of words on the board that could fit together to form compound words. Who can describe one of the words through movement? Come up and act out the word you chose. Now who can find another word on the list that could be added to the first word to form a compound word? Come up and describe your word through movement. Who can guess the compound word? Come up and act out that word. *(For example: Student 1 moves like the wind; Student 2 makes the actions of a mill grinding; Student 3 makes the shape and movements of a windmill.)*

3. *(Divide the class into three or four groups.)* Look at the list of

When you find a person with a word that goes with your word, get together and act out the compound word. This pair got together to form the word upstairs. ("Compound Words," Problem 1)

compound words on the board. Each group pick a compound word and think of a good sentence using your word. I am going to ask one group to say their sentence out loud, leaving a blank where the compound word fits in. How quickly can the other groups think of the right compound word and spell it out with their bodies?

4. *(Divide the class into groups.)* I am going to give each group a card with a word written on it. Think of different words that can be attached to the word on your card to form compound words. Have people in your group describe the words you think of through movement. We will watch each group when everyone is ready and try to guess all the compound words we see. *(Use words for the cards such as:* house, man, time, play, stairs, rain.)

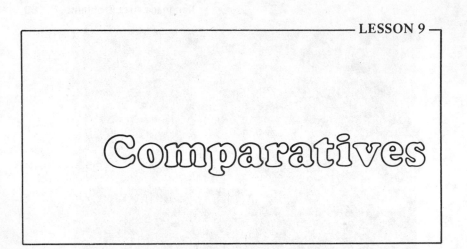

Comparatives

1. Can you make a thin shape? a thinner shape? the thinnest shape possible? Can you move as though you were sick? Now be sicker. Move the sickest way you possibly can. Try being tall. Can you be taller? Make the tallest movements possible. *(Continue with* pretty, ugly, silly, fat, thin, hot, cold, short, fast, slow, *etc.)*

2. Find two friends to work with. Think of a word to which you can add *-er* and *-est*. Each of you describe one of the words through nonlocomotor or locomotor movement. We will look at the trios and try to guess your words. *(For example: Student 1 might make a* big *shape; Student 2, a* bigger *shape; and Student 3, the* biggest *shape.)*

3. I am going to put a list of root words on the board. When you add *-er* or *-est* to some of the words, you must double the final consonant. For other words it is not necessary to double the final consonant. I will point to the words on the board one at a time. If the consonant should be doubled before adding the ending, touch two body parts to the floor. If the consonant is not doubled, stand still. Each time you touch two body parts to the floor try to think of a new combination of body parts to use. *(Use words such as* tall, big, small, fast, slow, short, fat, thin, hot, cold, mean, sick, weak, red, black, *etc.)*

    Variation: Include adjectives ending in y. *When you point to a word in which the last letter is changed to* i *before adding* -er

Can your trio think of a word to which you can add -er *and* -est? *Each of you describe one of the words.* This trio is describing small, smaller, smallest. ("Comparatives," Problem 2)

and -est, *the children could form the letter* i *or do some nonlocomotor action.*

4. With some adjectives we use the words *more* and *most* instead of adding *-er* or *-est*. I am going to write a list of adjectives on the board. When I point to a word that uses *more* or *most* for its comparative, make the shape of the letter *m*.

Or have the children perform a nonlocomotor action such as push, punch, bend, stretch, twist, *etc. Include words in your list such as:* beautiful, fun, wonderful, fantastic, crooked, circular, *etc.*

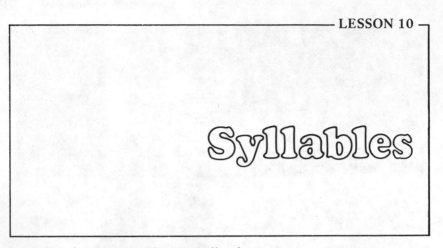

1. Let's take one word on our list *(use whatever words you are studying)*, say it slowly, and clap once for each syllable. Let's try another word. *(Continue clapping along with the children until all the words have been clapped through.)*

2. Instead of clapping the syllables, can you change your level on each syllable? We will have to say the word slowly so you will have time to change. *(Example:* Sat—*high level;* ur—*low level;* day—*medium level)*

3. Can you make a different shape for each syllable? Perhaps a twisted shape for the first syllable and a curved shape for the second syllable? Try angular, narrow, and wide shapes.

4. Can you punch your arm in a different direction for each syllable? Remember you can punch forward, backward, right, left, up, and down. Try another body part with another word. Try swinging; pushing and pulling; bending and stretching; twisting and untwisting; rocking or swaying.

5. Can you stamp your foot on each syllable? Try snapping your fingers; slapping your thighs; beating your chest; tapping your knees.

6. Can you take a step on each syllable? Try jumping; hopping; leaping; skipping; galloping; sliding. Say one word over and over again stepping, hopping, etc. on each syllable, letting the word move you across the room. Try moving through space in different directions.

7. Who can show me great big shapes for each syllable? Who can show me little tiny shapes for each syllable? Can you alternate big and little shapes on each syllable? Try making big shapes for the words with three or more syllables and little shapes for the words with two or fewer syllables.

8. Can you change your focus on each syllable? Now try doing that without moving your head. Just move your eyes in a different direction as you say each syllable out loud. *(This is an excellent exercise for strengthening the eye muscles.)*

9. Let's think about a word we are working on. Does it make you feel like moving sharply or smoothly? Maybe it feels like shaking or swinging. How many syllables are in the word *sharply*? Try making a sharp movement on each syllable. Can you make a smooth movement of each syllable in *smoothly*? a vibrating movement for each syllable in *shaking*? a swinging movement for each syllable in *swinging*? How do you feel like moving for *angry*? for *happy*? for *terrified*? for *silly*? for *laughing*? for *meanness*?

   Ask the students for other words. This problem provides exploration with the qualities of force while working on syllables.

10. Let's explore syllables and speed. Can you say each syllable very, very slowly and make one slow movement for each syllable? First try moving in your self space. Have a race with a friend to see who can finish *last*. Be sure to say your syllables clearly so you can check each other on whether you are dividing the word in the correct places. *(This is also a good exercise for balance.)*

    When you have gone through your words slowly, try saying the syllables quickly while you make a quick movement for each syllable. Be sure to enunciate your syllables and your movement. Don't let everything run together. Now try moving slowly and quickly through general space.

11. Every time you say a syllable, put one body part on the floor *(or desk, wall, etc.)*. If the word has three syllables, I should see only three body parts on the floor. For one syllable, there should be one body part. I will be able to tell if you have the

Let's think about a word we are working on. Does it make you feel like moving sharply or smoothly? Try making a different movement on each syllable. Using the word angry, these children chose to bend for *an-* and to punch for *-gry*. ("Syllables," Problem 9)

right number of syllables by the number of parts touching the floor.

You may call on students to tell what syllable corresponds to what body part. This will aid you in knowing if the students are dividing the words in the correct places.

12. Can you make up a syllable dance? *(You may want to use the word* routine, *phrase* or *pattern* in place of *dance.)* Pick a long word with many syllables or put several words together to form a sentence. Maybe you would like to start with your name. For each syllable, find a movement that you like. Put all the movements and syllables together and you will have a dance. Try to combine locomotor and nonlocomotor movement, different levels, directions, shapes, speeds, force, and range of movement.

Let's try the name *Harry S. Truman* together. What could you do for the first syllable *Har-?* A jump? For *-ry* let's try a low turn. Could you give a quick punch for *S?* Let's run four steps for *Tru-* and end up with a fall for *-man.* Now let's practice. Say each syllable as you move. We have:

HAR — RY   S   TRU — MAN
jump—low turn, quick punch, four runs—fall

Now try your own name. When you have practiced several times, sit down. When everyone is ready, we will show our syllable dances.

It is best to elicit ideas from the children for your example, but if you have trouble getting ideas, you can fall back on my example of Harry S. Truman.

13. *Problems 17-23 from "Spelling" can be used with syllables. Instead of spelling a word, children say each syllable as they do the movements described.*

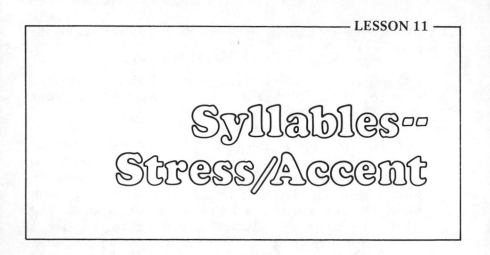

Syllables-- Stress/Accent

1. Can you say the word (*Saturday*), slowly dividing it into syllables? Now, say the first syllable more loudly than the second or third. Try saying the second syllable the loudest. Now say the third syllable the loudest. Which way sounded the best? The first way? When we say one syllable more loudly than the other, we call this stressing or accenting the syllable. In (*Saturday*) we accent the first syllable. Here is another word: (*watermelon*). Let us say the word slowly together. Clap on the syllable you think should be accented.

2. Listen for the accent in the word (*today*). Let us say the word together slowly, and stand up on the accented syllable. I am going to write other words on the board *(or say out loud)*, and we will say each word together. Change your level each time we say an accented syllable. *(Repeat each word several times.)*

3. Can you jump on the accented syllables and stay still on the unaccented syllables? punch? twist? turn around? strike? sit? fall? hop? push? pull? kick?

4. Take a big step on the accented syllable, and take short steps on the unaccented syllables.

5. Make a big nonlocomotor movement on the accented syllable, and make small movements on the unaccented syllables.

6. Change your direction on the accented syllable.

7. Hold still on the accented syllable and gallop on the unaccented syllable. Now run on the unaccented syllable; walk; slide; hop; leap; punch; twist; strike; dodge; turn.

8. Make a strong shape on the accented syllable, and make weak shapes on the unaccented syllables.

9. Make a very slow movement on the accented syllable, and make quick movements on the unaccented syllables. Can you make a quick movement on the accented syllables and slow movements on the other syllables?

10. Find a partner. One of you move just on the accented syllable, and the partner move on the other syllables. Change roles.

11. Let us play "Follow the Leader." I will say a word and make a movement on the accented syllable. You repeat the word and copy the movement. Then I will try a new word.

    For example: you would say di-rec-tion *and make a curled shape on* rec; *then the children would say* di-rec-tion *and try to repeat that shape as they say* rec. *After several words, you may want to choose a student leader. This is an excellent exercise for reinforcing the correctly accented syllables.*

12. *(Divide students into four to six groups. There should be four to six children in each group.)* Each group think of three words that you like. Find the accented syllable in each word. Create a movement for each syllable, making the accented syllables very special. Say the three words one after the other and do your movements as you say the words. Remember to use level, direction, range, force, speed, etc. We will look at each group and check the accented syllables.

    Also, comment on the elements of movement that gave variety to each group's dance. You might want to give the groups words that are accented on different syllables such as yesterday, today, tomorrow.

13. *(This problem uses equipment.)* Can you bounce the ball on the accented syllable? roll the ball? toss the ball? kick the ball? toss the beanbag? slide the beanbag to a partner? tap the wand

on the floor? roll the wand? toss the wand? balance the wand?
twirl the wand? toss the hoop? jump in or out of the hoop?
twirl the hoop? tap the hoop? jump over the rope? jump under
the rope? pull on the rope? do a trick while jumping rope?

Punctuation

1. Can you make the shape of each punctuation mark with your arm or arms as I say them out loud? Try your legs; an arm and a leg; your whole body.

2. Try making the shape of the punctuation marks I name on a high level; on a low level; on a medium level.

3. Can you make very tiny marks? giant size marks? medium marks?

4. Find a partner and together make the punctuation marks that have more than one part. *(Colon, semi-colon, exclamation mark, quotation marks.)*

5. Draw the punctuation marks in space with different body parts; on different levels; with big and small movements; with different force depending on the feeling each punctuation mark gives you; quickly and slowly.

6. Can you move your punctuation marks through space while walking, running, hopping, etc.? Think of what the punctuation mark implies and move accordingly. How would an exclamation mark move? [perhaps quickly, sharply and on a high level] How would a period move? [perhaps on a low level with starts and stops]

7. *(Divide the class into three to five groups.)* I'm going to give some word cards to each group. Make up a sentence with your

word cards. You do not have to use all of them. Hold your cards and arrange yourself in a line so that we can read your sentence. The rest of the groups will try to figure out how to punctuate your sentence by making the punctuation marks with their bodies and fitting themselves into the sentence. The group who punctuates the sentence correctly can be the next up with its sentence.

This problem provides good practice in sentence construction. Variations: If you are working with older students, have them write their sentences on the board. This will allow them to use more complex sentences. For younger children, write a simple sentence on the board without punctuation. Ask them to form the correct punctuation mark for the sentence.

8. *(Divide students into groups of five or seven.)* I am going to give each group a card with two words on it. *(Use combinations such as* I am, you will, do not, *etc.)* Get together in your group and spell out the contraction for your words. Do not forget to form the punctuation mark used in contractions. Can the other groups guess what your original words were? Did you punctuate the contraction correctly?

Stories

These problems can be done with reading groups, other small groups, pairs, or the whole class.

1. I am going to read a story out loud, and while I am reading, listen carefully to the action in the story. When I am finished, I will ask you to recreate the story through movement. You will only be able to use your body, not your voice. *(You may only want to read a passage or chapter depending on the length of the story and the age of the children.)*

   What people or animals in the story do we need to recreate? Do we need any buildings, objects, plants, or machines? Who would like to be what? Let us go over what happened in the story. Are you ready to act it out? Remember, no voices!

   You might want to give cues if the children become confused. The movement story could be performed for other children in the class. Another group may want to try to recreate the story, or the first group may want to rehearse it a few times to make the story clear.

2. Choose a paragraph or section of a story that we've read and you would like to recreate through movement.

   See that each child has a different section and together they recreate the whole story or section. It is always fun for the children to have the teacher take part.

When your paragraph comes in the story, read it out loud and think of different ways you could act it out. When we have read the story, we will start over again and dance the story. Be sure to end in a shape and hold it so the next person will know when to begin.

3. Let us think of a story that we all know well. *(Talk over a fairy tale or favorite book.)* I am going to divide the class into two different groups. Each group will have its own cast of characters. *(Assign characters to each group.)*

   The first group will begin to act out the story, but as soon as I clap my hands, they must sit down and the second group will pick up where they left off. We will keep changing groups each time I clap my hands. Do you think you can keep the story going in the right order?

4. *(Divide the class into groups.)* I am going to give each group a section of a story. Choose a narrator for your group. Recreate your story through movement as your narrator reads aloud the story. Take your time with the actions. Do not just panto-mime the actions, but add levels and directions, range, force, and speed to your movements. If you are a cat, you do not have to walk on all fours. You could stand on your head, and we would know you are a cat if your movements are the slow, sinuous, twisting of a cat stalking or the quick, clawing, arched actions of a cat pouncing. When you have your section ready, we will put the story together in order. Then we will discuss what we saw.

5. *You will need materials for this problem: newspapers and safety pins or tape, large paper bags, crayons and scissors, hoops, balls, beanbags and wands, elastic, volleyball nets, or pieces of fabric may be used.* Make four different props out of your materials. Now create a simple movement story with a beginning, middle, and end using your props. We will show the stories to each other and try to guess the plot. *The props may be made in art class and used later. You may do this problem using groups, pairs, or individuals. The children also enjoy exchanging props and creating stories.*

6. *(Put names of animals, characters, objects, buildings, things in nature, etc. on individual cards.)* I am going to shuffle these

cards and have you each choose one card. Now let us count off and form groups. *(There should be four to six students in each group.)*

Get together in your group, and create a movement story using the characters on your cards. When you are ready, sit down; then we will show each story and guess the plot.

Variation: Do not discuss the movement story after the children have seen it. Have each child make up a story about what he or she saw and write it down. Then read all the different stories and discuss them. It is best to just have one group perform a day. This is a challenging activity for the children's imaginations. For example, one group may get the names of four buildings and a plant, while another has three things in nature and two machines.

7. *Write three words on the board such as these examples:* coming, meeting, parting; thinking, working, resting; silly, scared, relieved; look, find, lose; sad, angry, happy. *Elicit some ideas from your students.*

Make up a story using these three words. The first word will be the beginning idea, the second word the middle idea, and the third word the ending idea. Remember to have a climax in your story. It may be in any section. When you have thought of a story, translate it into movement and show it to the class.

You may wish to use groups or pairs or trios for this problem. Discuss the construction of the story and where the climax was placed.

8. Draw a picture. Then give that picture to a friend or another group. Ask them to create a movement story to illustrate your picture.

9. Write a story *(or read a story)* and leave off the ending. Choose a group to think of an ending for your story, and ask them to describe the ending through movement.

It is also fun to have three to five groups work on an ending simultaneously. Then you will have many different endings for the same story.

10. Pretend you are acting out your story on film. When I say *fast*, the film will speed up. Can you move twice as fast as you normally move and still act out the story? When I say *slow*, the film will slow down. Can you move half as fast as you normally move? Let's try.

11. *Read a story to the class that deals with emotions. Fables are good for this activity because they are short, and children enjoy discussing the moral. After you have read a story, perhaps Aesop's fable "The Fox and the Crow," encourage movement exploration with questions similar to the following.*

    What was the story saying? [Do not trust flatterers.] How do you feel when someone flatters you? Can you show me through movement? What would your body shape be like? your chest? neck? arms? head? Where would your focus be? What kind of pathway would you make? How do you feel when someone tricks you? *(Elicit personal experiences from the children that relate to the story.)*

    Now, instead of moving like a person, let's move like a big, black crow. How would you move your wings and beak and feet? How would a proud crow who is showing-off move? How would the crow move after the fox had tricked her? Show me. *(Continue with similar questions about the fox.)*

    This activity has several different purposes: to assist the children in understanding the essence of the character; to encourage the children to relate the characters' experiences to their own experiences; to give the children the opportunity to act out and understand feelings that they may have been unable to previously. This is a very therapeutic activity.

12. *Storybooks may be used in conjunction with other problems in this book to help motivate movement and reinforce the academic concept you are studying. There are many books (see Bibliography) on numbers, the alphabet, colors, plants, animals, etc. that could be read and discussed before or during the movement class. The pictures in these books are very helpful for giving size and shape ideas to children. They may also help you think of other movement questions to ask in addition to the ones included in this book.*

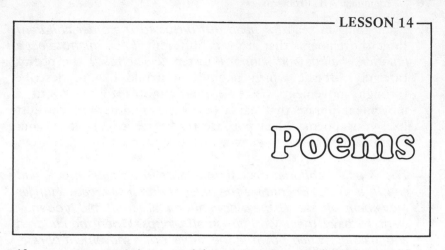

Poems

If you are studying special poems that deal with machines, emotions, seasons, holidays, etc., you may want to do some of the problems in this book that deal specifically with those subjects. The following problems deal with poetry in general.

1. *(For this problem choose short poems with much action and many movement words. See the Bibliography for ideas.)* I am going to read a poem. Listen carefully to the rhythm and the words. *(After you have read the poem, continue.)* On what level does this poem make you feel like moving? Could you move in several directions? What locomotor movement could you do? Is it a poem with strong or weak force? Do the words tumble out quickly or move slowly? Think about those things as I read the poem again. Show me all the ways the poem makes you move. *(You may want to divide the class in half to show the solutions.)*

2. *(For this problem choose poems with definite mood changes.)* I am going to read a poem *(or ask a student to read one)*, and I want you to listen carefully to the rhythm and words and to think of how the poem makes you feel. I will read it twice; then I want you to move in ways that describe the feeling with which the poem left you.

   This problem deals with more abstract thinking than the first problem. Instead of acting out the poem literally, the children should try first to understand the overall mood of the poem. Then they can attempt to translate this mood into movement.

3. I am going to read *(or hand out dittos to the older children)* three short poems that are very different. *(You might select a limerick, haiku, and sonnet.)* Listen to *(or read)* the poems carefully. Decide which poem you would like to describe through movement. Take a few minutes to work out a movement phrase that has a beginning, middle, and end just like your poem. When you are ready, we will look at your poem dance and try to guess which poem you selected.

The younger children may simply start in a shape, move, and end in a shape. Encourage the older children to create a longer movement phrase. If the older children are inhibited, you may want to have them work in small groups. When the children are guessing which poem is the subject of a movement phrase, ask them to give reasons for their guesses.

4. *(Divide the class in half.)* Each half of the class will have a poem to work on. You may work in pairs or individually. I will give each pair or individual one line of the poem. Think about the rhythm, mood, and words of your poem, and then create a movement pattern to describe your line of poetry. Say your line out loud as you move. When everyone is ready, we will listen to and watch as the pairs or individuals say their lines and do their patterns in the correct order to create the whole poem.

Some points you may want to bring out in discussion are: Did the movement seem to match the words? What different elements of movement were used to help create the rhythm, mood, and meaning of each line? Did the poem make sense when all the lines were put together? Sometimes it will and sometimes it won't. It is difficult to take lines out of context and then put them together and have them make sense. The emphasis and rhythm changes with each individual interpretation. However, the results are interesting and provide stimuli for lively discussions.

5. *(Divide the class into small groups.)* I am going to give you a ditto sheet with poems on it. *(Have at least as many poems as groups.)* Read the poems in your group, and pick one that you would like to describe through movement. Choose one person to be narrator. The narrator will read the poem as the rest of

the group performs. Remember to start in a shape and end in a shape so that the rest of us will know when you are beginning and finishing your movement poem. Use all the elements of movement. Try to capture the mood and rhythm of the poem as well as the meaning. When everyone is ready, sit down and we will watch each group.

6. I would like you to compose a poem. *(In a style you have been studying perhaps.)* When you have finished, create a movement phrase for your poem and perform it for the class. Can you recite the poem as you move, or would you like a friend to recite it for you? Perhaps, you would rather read the poem first and then move.

You stupid scarecrow!
Under your very
Stick-feet
Birds are stealing beans!
Yayu

("Poems," Problem 8)

Reprinted by permission from *Japanese Haiku*, by Peter Beilenson. Copyright © 1955, 1956 by Peter Pauper Press, Mount Vernon, New York.

*Discuss the poem and movement with the class. You might
decide to have the children write poems one day and to create
movement the next.*

7. Find a partner. Each of you write a short, complimentary
   poem about the other. Exchange poems and create a movement pattern to go with your poem. You will be composing a
   dance to yourself! Show your dances to each other and discuss
   how you felt while you were dancing about yourself.

8. I am going to read a haiku and I want you to listen to the
   rhythm and mood of the poem. *(Read the haiku once, and
   then ask questions about the imagery, mood, shape, space,
   tempo, force, and levels used in the haiku.)*

   Now I am going to give each group of people a haiku. Read the
   poem together. Then talk about all the things we discussed
   with the first haiku. When you have a good understanding of
   the haiku, create a dance that describes it. When you are
   ready: I will read the haiku; your group will perform; then I
   will read the haiku again. After that we will discuss what we
   saw. *(Reading the haiku before and after the dance is helpful
   in relating the words to the movement.)*

   *Variation: It is also interesting to give each group the same
   haiku and discuss the results. The groups will create many
   different dances for the same poem. The children also enjoy
   writing their own haiku for which they can compose dances.*

Emotions

1. How would you feel if someone gave you a million dollars? Can you show me through movement? What level are you dancing on? What kind of force are you using? What directions are you moving in? At what speed are you going? What is your range of movement? Think of all these things as you are expressing your feelings.

2. How would you feel if you didn't get any summer vacation? Try showing me your feelings through movement. *(Again ask the children to think of the different ways in which they are moving.)*

    How did your movement differ from your movement when you received a million dollars? Were you on a different level? [Perhaps low instead of high.] How did the force change? [Maybe weaker.] Did your movement change speed? [Probably slowed down.] Was your range of movement smaller? Our emotions very definitely affect our movement.

    Some other situations you might present to elicit emotions are: an earthquake beginning, a bear chasing you, all A's on your report card, your sister or brother gets a new bicycle and you do not, your first day at a new school, your house is on fire, a big bully pushes you in the mud, you've just eaten 20 pies in a pie eating contest, you don't get any presents on your birthday, you have to recite a poem in front of 200 people, etc.

How would you feel if a big bully pushed you in the mud? ("Emotions," Problem 2)

3. I'm going to say a word and I want you to make a face that expresses that word. Just use your face. The word is *(happy)*. *(Use words such as* sad, scared, silly, angry, discouraged, jealous, shy, bored, nervous, terrified, upset, excited, lonely, *etc.)* Can you express that word with just your arms? your legs? your whole body? Instead of doing a lot of movement, freeze like a photograph in a shape that expresses the word I gave you. Try another shape on a different level. Let's look at some of these shapes.

4. Who can name an emotion for the class to express through movement? As you move through space, try different loco-motor movements. Can you express this emotion while walk-ing? while galloping? jumping? skipping? Can you express it while bending? while twisting? turning? Can you make your movements bigger? smaller? stronger? weaker? faster? slower? Let's try another emotion.

This problem is more difficult than the first two because, whereas in those problems the children allowed their feelings to dictate their movements, here they have to try to express the emotion while moving in ways that may feel contra-dictory. For example: You are asking them to move at a low level or with weak force or slow speed while expressing happiness. Normally, one would not move those ways to express happiness.

(Discuss with the children how it feels to move in ways that seem to contradict the emotion.) Can you think of a situation where you might be very happy but could not get up and jump around? *(You are sick in bed, but the doctor tells you that you will be well soon.)* Can you think of other contradictory situations? Let's try them.

5. Find a partner. Decide on an emotion you would like to portray (or pick one out of a hat). Working together, can you find a shape that expresses your emotion? Try some different shapes, and when you have a shape that expresses your emotion best, freeze like statues. Let's go around the room and see how many statues we can name correctly.

6. Body language means talking with your body instead of your voice. Let's see how good you are at understanding body

Can the group facing the card express the emotion written on it for the other group to guess? ("Emotions," Problem 6)

language. Form two lines facing each other. *(See Problem 8 in "Synonyms, Antonyms, Homonyms.")* I will hold up an emotion word for one group to see, and they will express that emotion in their self space using body language. How quickly can the other group guess the emotion? *(Continue, alternating between groups.)*

7. Let's divide into groups. I'm going to give each group a card with an emotion written on it. I will give you time to work in your groups on your emotion dance (routine, pattern, etc.). Remember to use different levels, range, force, speed, directions, etc. When you have finished practicing, sit down. Then we'll watch one group at a time, and try to guess the emotion they are expressing.

8. I will give each group a card with a situation written on it. *(See Problem 2, "Emotions," for examples of situations.)* Act out the situation in your group, and the rest of the class will try to name an emotion they see expressed in your movement. Perhaps there will be more than one emotion portrayed.

You might also ask the class to write down situations on cards and then have the groups pick cards out of a hat. Remind the children again of the elements of movement and encourage them to use as many variations as possible. Ask the children to describe the different elements used by a group and to explain how the movement used helped them to name the emotions.

PART II

MATHEMATICS PROBLEMS

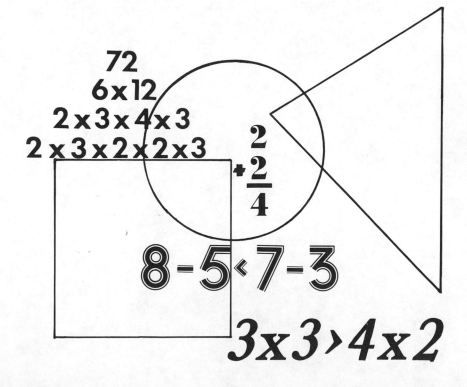

Math Readiness

Big and Little

1. Can you make a big shape— a shape as big as an elephant? Now try a tiny shape—a shape an ant might make. Let us go around the room. Each of you make a body shape, and the rest of us will decide if it is a big shape or a little shape. Then you can tell us if we are correct.

2. Look at the two pictures I am holding up. First make the shape of the object that is big; then make the shape of the object that is little. *(Use simple shapes and try many pairs.)*

Long and Short

3. Can you take long, giant steps across the room? Now, try short steps coming back the other way. *(Try jumps, hops, runs, etc.)*

4. *(Hold up pictures with pairs of objects, one of which is long and one short. Pictures of pencils, socks, string, paper, tables, and similar objects work well.)* Look at the pair of objects in this picture. If the object I point to is long, take one long step away from your chair. If the object I point to is short, take a short step toward your chair.

Tall and Short

5. Can you reach for the ceiling? Really stretch your arms and legs. When you do that you are tall. Now crouch down a little

and make a short shape with your body. Stretch tall again. Relax and become short. Can you move to this rhyme?

I'm tall.
I'm short.
I'm very, very tall.
I'm very, very short.
Sometimes I'm tall.
Sometimes I'm short.
Guess what I am now!

6. Can you name some animals that move on the ground? Good. Now, which ones are short and which ones are tall? *(You may want to show a picture book with animals of different heights grouped together.)* Let's make the shape of a tall animal first and then the shape of a short animal. Can your animal move around the room? *(Continue, working on many animal shapes.)*

Low and High

7. Can you put your arms higher than your head? Now put your arms lower than your head. Can you put your head lower than your knees? Can you put your toes higher than your head? *(Continue, asking similar questions.)*

8. Can you make a body shape on a low level—a shape that is close to the ground? Can you make a shape on a high level—a shape close to the ceiling? Try a different low level shape. Now try a different high level shape. Let us look at some of the shapes and guess whether they are high or low. Now try making a high jump. Can you make a low jump?

Wide and Narrow

9. Can you stretch your arms and legs out to the side and make a very wide shape? Try making a giant X. Now bring all your body parts together and make a narrow shape. Make a shape like a toothpick. Can you make another wide shape and move that shape across the room? When you get to the other side, make a narrow shape and move back to where you started.

10. Let us make some lanes with our desks, as boundaries. We will make some lanes narrow and some wide. Move between the

desks. When you reach a narrow lane, you will have to make a narrow shape in order to fit through. When you reach a wide lane, you will be able to make a wide shape.

Many and Few

11. Hold up many fingers. Now, can you hold up just a few? Can you touch many body parts to the floor? Touch just a few parts to the floor. Take many hops forward. Try a few hops backward.

12. I would like to see many people walk over to the chalkboard. I will tap the heads of just a few people who will run to the bookcase. Many people sit down. A few stand up. Do you see many people standing up or just a few? Many people jump up and down. A few people stretch to the ceiling.

This is a good lesson in group cooperation. If all the children begin moving instead of many, some should stop. If many children begin moving instead of a few, some should stop. This becomes a game between the teacher and the class. Try other movement ideas.

Not Any or None

13. Can you make a circle with your arms? Now put something in your circle, like your head or foot or knee. Take the body part out of the circle, and you have nothing in the circle. There is not anything left in it. Make a square with your legs. Put one or more body parts into your square. Now, show me an empty square; a square with no body parts in it. *(Continue with other shapes.)*

14. Let's play "Simon Says." When I say, "Simon says do this," do what I am doing. When I just say, "Do this," you do nothing. There should not be any movements when I just say, "Do this."

Have the students perform some simple motions, such as stretching, moving their legs, bending their elbows, etc. Frequently say simply "Do this" in place of "Simon Says" and reinforce those students who do nothing.

Can you put your hands, above your head? ("Math Readiness," Problem 15)

Positional Concepts

15. Stand *in front* of your desk. Can you stand *behind* your desk? Can you stand *beside* your desk? Stand in the *middle* of the row of desks. Stand *between* your desk and your neighbor's desk. Move *around* your desk. Put your hand *on top* of your desk. Can you put your hand *under* your desk? Put your hand *in* your desk. Put your fingers *above* your chair. Now try putting your fingers *below* your chair. Can you put your fingers *through* a space in the chair?

16. *(Set up a simple obstacle course with ropes, desks, chairs, etc.)* Let's play "Follow the Leader." Listen to my directions. Go over the first rope and under the second rope. Go through the chairs and around the desk. Go behind the wastebasket and in front of the bookcase. Move beside the chalkboard until you come to the door. *(Try to let everyone move past one obstacle before you name the next.)*

Numbers

Most of the problems in this chapter can be done using Roman numerals instead of Arabic numerals.

1. Can you make the shape of a number between 1 and 9? Use your whole body.

2. Can you make the shape of the number that tells how old you are?

3. Can you make a 2 with your hands? arms? legs? one arm and one leg? two legs and an arm? *(Continue with other numbers and body parts.)*

4. What numbers can you make with a partner? *(Have the children look at each other's solutions.)*

5. What numbers can you make with three people? with four people? Can the whole class get together and make one giant number between 1 and 9? *(This takes some organizing, but it is a good exercise in spatial awareness and group cooperation.)*

6. Can you make a *3* (or any single-digit numeral) standing up? sitting down? kneeling? lying down? *(Use of* levels.*)*

7. Can you make a giant number? a tiny number? a medium-sized number? *(Use of* range.*)*

What numbers can you make with a partner? These children are making the number 4. ("Numbers," Problem 4)

8. Can you show me all the even numbers between 1 and 10? all the odd numbers between 1 and 10?

9. Can your number hop across the room and keep its shape? Who can show me a skipping *1*? a leaping *4*? a walking *5*? a sliding *8*? *(Combine different locomotor movements with different numbers.)*

10. Can your number twist? turn? push? pull? stretch? bend? punch? Show me how you can stay in your number shape and do all those nonlocomotor movements.

11. Can you make a frozen *0*? When I give the signal, melt into another number, freeze, and let us guess what your new number is. *(Use of flow.)*

12. Can your number move backwards? forwards? sideways right? sideways left? *(Use of direction.)*

13. I am going to turn your knee into a crayon. Show me how you can write *(name a number)* in the air with your knee; with

your leg; head; elbow; hip; shoulder; back. Let us try another number, and this time trace the number on the floor with all those different body parts.

Continue using the space in front, in back, above, underneath, to the side, etc. This problem deals with spatial relationships, body parts, and numbers.

14. Let us make number kites. Turn your body into the shape of your favorite number. Now let the wind catch your number kite and fly it through the air. The wind becomes stronger and stronger. Remember to keep your shape. Now the wind is dying down. You are falling slowly back to the ground until you land gently on the grass. Are you still in the shape of your number? *(Use of weak and strong force)*

15. How many different ways can you make *(name a number)*. *(This could be a continuous contest.)*

16. Find a partner and trace a number on your partner's back. Can your partner guess the number you traced? Now let your partner trace a number on your back.

How many different ways can you make the number 22? These children are using Roman numerals to show XXII. ("Numbers," Problem 15)

17. Find a partner. One of you is a pencil and one is a writer. The writer is going to stand behind the pencil with his or her hands on the pencil's shoulders. Now guide your pencil slowly in the shape of a number. Your pencil's feet will draw the number on the floor as you move him or her around. Can your pencil guess the number you wrote? Go slowly so the pencil has time to think. Try being a pencil with your eyes closed. *(A good activity for developing kinesthetic awareness.)*

18. Find a partner and make a number with two digits. Try making the number on different levels; move in different directions; change speeds; try other locomotor movements.

For problems 19 and 20 divide the class into small groups.

19. Make a number in the hundreds or thousands with your group. Do not forget the comma if you need one. What is the highest number you can make with your group? the lowest number? the highest even and odd number? the lowest even and odd number? Let us compare groups.

20. Make a multi-digited number in your group. Can you move the number across the floor and stay together? Can you move the number on different levels? in different directions? with different speeds? with weak and strong force? hopping or jumping? *(This is quite a challenge in group cooperation.)* Now let us try to guess each group's number.

Problems 21-23 may be done in small groups, in pairs, or by individuals. If done in pairs or with individuals, direct a student or pair of students to form each number. Then have the class call out the number before the next number is formed. You can write the numbers on the board as they are guessed.

21. Pick a group member's telephone number and form the numbers in the right order with your bodies. Do not forget the hyphen. If you move quickly, we will be able to make everyone's telephone number.

22. Try writing a group member's street number. If there are more people than numbers, get together in pairs or trios to form the address. If the street you live on is also a number, include that

in your solution. We'll guess the addresses when everyone is ready.

23. In your groups, form today's date with numbers. Put the month in the form of a number along with the day and year. *(After these are shown, continue.)* Now make up a month, day, and year. Perhaps you can think of a famous date we have been studying or a holiday or your birthday. We will guess the secret dates when everyone is ready. If your group finishes before another group, think of a second date.

Problems 24 and 25 use balls and jump ropes.

24. Can you bounce the ball in the shape of a *2*? Can you roll the ball in the shape of a *4*? Can you dribble the ball with your feet in the shape of a *6*? Can you toss and catch the ball while you draw the number *8* on the floor with your feet? with your heel? with your toe? with one hand? with your back? with your buttocks?

25. Can you make the shape of a number with your jump rope and walk along the rope, tracing the number you made? Can you trace the number while running? crawling? sliding? hopping? walking backwards?

Counting

1. Let us go through the numbers from 1 to 10 and try to use as many body parts to form a number as the number designates. For example, for the number *1* we will use one body part to form the number.

2. I am going to call out numbers. Put the same number of body parts on the floor as the number I call out. When I say *2*, you should touch two body parts to the floor.

   You can easily spot children who are having trouble remembering how much the number represents. Fingers and toes may be used for higher numbers.

3. I am going to say a number. *(Or write it on the board.)* Can you take as many steps forward as the number names? steps backward? hops? jumps? runs? skips? rolls? punches? twists? turns? kicks? stretches? bends? swings? *(Combine the movements with different directions for older children.)*

4. I am going to draw some objects on the board. *(Or hold up pictures of different numbers of objects or tape pieces of colored paper on the board, etc.)* Count the number of objects you see and make the shape of that number with your body or body parts.

5. As I clap my hands, count the claps. When I am finished, make the shape of the last number you counted.

Can you touch 2 body parts to the floor? 1 body part? ("Counting," Problem 2)

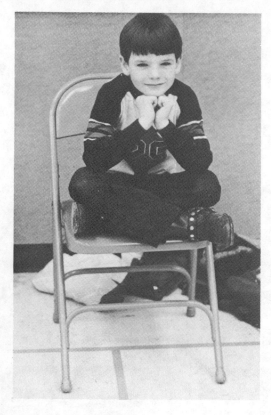

Can you touch 0 body parts to the floor? ("Counting, Problem 2)

Try rapping on the desk, bouncing a ball, snapping fingers, stamping feet, slapping thighs, clucking tongues, etc. Ask the children to make sounds for counting.

6. Everyone whose address begins with the number 2 come to the front of the room. Those left at their desks count the people standing up and make the shape of the number with your body. *(Continue with other address numbers or telephone numbers.)*

7. Who would like to hop a certain number of times for us to count? When the hopper has stopped hopping, make the shape of the number you counted. *(Try other locomotor and nonlocomotor movements to count.)*

8. Let us play an echo game. Someone will make a sound. *(See*

Problem 5, "Counting," for sound ideas.) Count the number of sounds the person makes; then repeat the same number of sounds just like an echo. Try to keep in time with your classmates as you repeat the sounds.

9. *(This is a good review of the previous problems.)* I am going to hold up a group of objects. *(Or hold up a picture of a group of objects).* Count the number of objects you see. How many different ways can you show me the number you counted?

   These are some possible solutions: make shape of Arabic or Roman numeral; hold up number of body parts; make sounds with equipment, instruments, voice or body parts (one sound for each object); make a locomotor or nonlocomotor movement for each object; get a group of students together to represent objects; trace the number in the air or on the floor; form an equation whose solution is the number of objects counted.

10. *Form the class into a circle, and count off by numbers—from 1-5, from 6-10, or by 10s to 50. Count off by whatever numbers you want to practice, using about five numbers.*

    I am going to hold up a certain number of fingers. *(Or a picture of several objects.)* If you have the same number, run around the circle and back to your home spot as fast as you can. If I hold up five fingers, all the number *5s* will run around the circle.

    Variations: (a) Runners try to tag the person in front of them as they run. There is no penalty for being tagged. (b) Call out a movement before holding up your fingers. The children must move that way around the circle. You might say "backward walk" and hold up two fingers. The number 2s have to walk backwards around the circle. (c) Use fractions and pictures instead of fingers to represent fractions. For example, hold up a card with the number ½ written on it or on which a half-filled glass is drawn.

11. *Make a large cardboard grid with numbers on it, draw a grid on the floor or wall, or tape circles with numbers in them on the floor. You will also need a spinner with pictures containing*

Diagram 3. ("Counting," Problem 11)

different numbers of objects. The pictures should correspond to the Arabic numerals on the grid. Use any numbers you wish the children to practice. Instead of numbers you might use Roman numerals. (See Diagram 3.)

Find some friends to play "Number Twisto." Have someone spin the spinner as you take turns moving. Whatever picture the spinner lands on, you have to count the number of objects and find the matching number on the grid. Then put a body part on that number and stay there. Each time it is your turn, put another body part on the numeral of your spin. Whoever is able to make the last play is the next spinner.

12. *The class may do this activity as a whole or divide into groups. If groups are used, let them watch each other perform.*

Each person pick two numbers between 1 and 10 and keep them to yourself. *(You may want to use numbers up to 20 or 30 if working with the whole class.)* I am going to count out loud starting with 1. Count along with me silently until I reach the first number you picked. Then shout out your number and make a quick, interesting movement. Freeze in your shape until I reach your second number. Shout out your second number and make a new shape. I will repeat all the numbers three times, going just a little faster each time. Can you keep up with me and come in on your numbers at the right time with a shout and a shape? Let's try.

Variations: (a) Clap instead of counting. The children have to count the claps to themselves and come in at the right time.

Give them a good starting signal so that they will start together—"Ready, go, (clap)." (b) Take away all sounds so that the children are keeping the rhythm by themselves. Give them four claps or counts to set the rhythm—"Ready, 1, 2, 3, 4, 1." The children begin on your second 1. The rhythm should be slow the first several times you play the game. (c) Try counting in another base. (d) Count in multiples of 3, 4, etc.

13. *Make one deck of cards with numbers in whatever range you wish, perhaps 1-15. Make another deck of cards with action words such as* crawl, hop, turn, fall, melt, punch, *etc. Each deck should have the same number of cards. Shuffle both decks separately. This activity may be played with the class as a whole, in partners, or in small groups.*

    I am going to ask you to pick one card from the number deck and one from the action deck. Can you perform the action as many times as your number card specifies? We will all count with you as you do it. Now let's try three sets of action and number cards so that you will have a movement phrase *(for example: 3 jumps, 8 crawls, 5 punches).* This time we won't count out loud. I will clap *(beat drum, snap, etc.)* the number of times it will take to do each action. *(For the previous example, you would clap sixteen times at a moderate tempo.)* Count to yourself as I clap. Try to change actions on the right number. End your movement exactly as I end my clapping. Let's have everybody try it.

14. Someone pick a number between 1 and 20 (perhaps 16). Find a space in the room to stand in. As we count to 16, move away from your space and then back to your space in the time it takes us to count the number. Try to get back to exactly the same space just as we say "16." Try many different kinds of movements, speeds, levels, and directions. How far can you move away and still be back in time? Let's try another number.

    Variations: (a) Do not count out loud. Keep the rhythm by clapping or beating. (b) Work in partners. One person moves through general space, while the other person stays in his or her self space and moves nonlocomotively for the specified number of counts. Switch positions for each new number. (c) Try counting in multiples or other bases.

15. *For this activity you need to set up an ordinal obstacle course. It can be as simple or complex as desired. If you use your classroom, just put a few more items around like an extra wastebasket and line up some spare chairs. If you use the gym, you might set up a course similar to that in Diagram 4. If you have enough equipment, set up two courses so that children will not be waiting too long in lines.*

I am going to give each person *(or pair, if there are two courses)* commands using ordinal numbers. Follow the commands and see how quickly and correctly you can get through our ordinal obstacle course. I might say: bounce the first ball once, toss the third beanbag twice, crawl around the sixth and eighth wand, roll on the third mat, and jump in and out of the fifth hoop. Are you ready? Here is the first command.

Give new commands for each person or pair. Have the other children check those going through the course. To make things move faster, give each child a task sheet with commands written out and have partners check each other. In the classroom use commands such as: crawl around the fourth

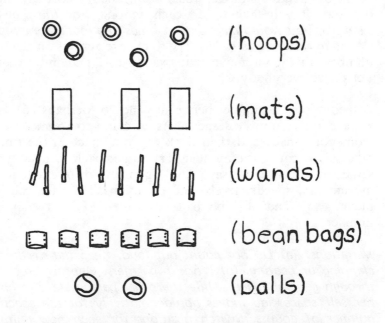

Diagram 4. An ordinal obstacle course. ("Counting," Problem 15)

desk in the first row, jump to the third piece of chalk on the chalk tray, walk backwards to the second wastebasket, etc.

16. *Have the children act out number rhymes and songs using body shapes, body parts, or bodies to represent the numbers. See the Bibliography for books containing these rhymes.*

Problems 17 and 18 use simple equipment such as balls, jump ropes, beanbags, and hoops.

17. I am going to put a number on the board *(or hold one up)*. Jump rope as many times as the number names; bounce the ball; toss the beanbag; twirl the hoop.

18. Make the shape of a number with your rope. Now, walk along the rope and trace the number you made. Can you take just as many steps as the number names. *(This is challenging but possible.)*

Sets

1. Do you know what the word *set* means? A *set* is a group of objects that are alike. What are some sets that you can think of? [Set of dishes, books, animals, chairs, pencils, etc.] Good, now who would like to describe one of those sets through movement? Choose some friends to help you. *(When the set is ready, continue.)* Can the rest of you give a name to the set? Guess what objects the students are making. How many objects are in the set? Who would like to make a new set of objects for us to count and name? Can anyone think of a way to show a set with no members? This is called the *empty set.*

2. *(This activity deals with matching sets. Use simple chalkboard drawings or cutouts and a flannel board, as shown in Diagram 5.)* How many dogs do you see? Make the number with your body. How many bones do you see? Make the number with your body. Are there as many bones as dogs? Could each dog have a bone? If you think each dog could have a bone, make the shape of a bone. If you do not think there are enough bones for dogs, make the shape of a sad dog. Ready, go! *(Continue with other sets that have a one-to-one correspondence.)*

3. I need three volunteers to form a line. Can you each make a shape on a low level? Now, three more volunteers come up and form a line facing the first line. Each of you make a shape on a high level. How can we show that these two sets match? [One way would be to have two people at a time return to their chairs. There would be no people left over.] Let us try some

Diagram 5. ("Sets," Problem 2)

other one-to-one matching. Who can give us ideas for two matching sets? Let's try some of the ideas.

Some possible ideas: six children making curved shapes, and six children making angular shapes, or four strong shapes and four weak shapes. When the sets are matched up, no members are left remaining. Older children enjoy getting into groups with an even number of people and creating matching sets for their classmates to view.

4. Let us compare the quantity of two sets. First we need to make a lot of different sets. Either create a set by yourself (a set with one member) or ask one or more friends to join you in creating a set. We should have many sets with different numbers of objects in them. When you have decided how to describe your set through movement, sit down. Now, I will ask two sets at a time to stand up and show the set you created. Look at the first pair of sets. Is the set on the left greater than, less than, or the same as the set on the right? Is the set on the right greater than, less than, or the same as the set on the left? *(Continue until all students have shown their sets.)*

Variations: (a) Ask the students to compare the sets orally. For example: The set of oranges is greater than the set of strong shapes. (b) Compare left to right. If the set on the left is greater, make a big shape; if it is less, make a tiny shape; if it is the same, make a medium-sized shape or an equal sign. (c) Use mathematical problems such as: 36 − 4   10; 20 + 25   30 + 16; 5 × 10   5 × 20; 8 ÷ 4   14 ÷ 7. Have the children make the correct sign with their bodies.

5. Now we are going to compare the quantity of more than two sets. *(Have the class create sets of different members as in Problem 4.)* I am going to ask three sets to stand up. Is the middle set greater, less than, or the same as the set on the left? Is it greater, less than, or the same as the set on the right? *(Continue with the variations described in Problem 4.)*

6. Who would like to get some friends and make a set of four chairs? Now I need some people to make a set of four trees. Can these sets be matched? Good. We call these two sets

Can your group form equivalent sets? These two sets are equivalent because they each contain the same number of objects — three — but the objects are different — three strong shapes in one set and three weak shapes in the other set. ("Sets," Problem 6)

equivalent. They have the same number of objects, but the objects in each set are different. What groups can show us other equivalent sets?

7. Who would like to make the shape of a ball? I need two balls. Who can make the shape of a candy cane? I need two candy canes. I also need two rabbits. Now one ball, one rabbit, and one candy cane come over here. The other ball, rabbit, and candy cane go over there. Do these sets match? Are the same objects in each set? Good. These sets are *equal.* There are the same number of objects and the same objects in each set. *(Change the order of the objects so that one set consists of a ball, candy cane, and rabbit and the other set has a rabbit, ball and candy cane.)* Now, are these sets equal? Do they still have the same number and the same objects as each other? They are still equal. Let's get into groups and create other equal sets.

8. *(If you have access to balls, beanbags, hoops, etc., use them, as shown in Diagram 6. Otherwise, you can use books, chairs, tables, erasers, etc.)* Can I have two people making shapes on different levels near the four hoops and three balls? I am going to ask the rest of you to answer questions about *more* and *less.* If one set has *more* than another set, make a giant shape. If one set has *less* than another set, then make a tiny shape. Are there more or less balls than hoops? Are there more or less hoops than people? Would each child be able to have more than one hoop? Let's try some new sets. This time stretch for *more* and bend for *less. (Continue, trying other nonlocomotor movements.)*

Diagram 6. ("Sets," Problem 8)

9. Everyone in the class think of an object you would like to describe through movement. You might be a machine, animal, person, vehicle, or object in nature. When everyone has thought of something and practiced his or her idea, we will go on. Now, I am going to describe a set, and all the objects that would fit in that set will make their shapes and move. The rest of us will look at the set and guess the objects to see if everyone belongs in the set.

Describe sets in terms such as these: They eat food; You ride on them; They are bigger than a breadbox; They can run; You put things in them. This activity could introduce union and intersection of sets. The children's objects may fit in several sets. You may wish to bring out in discussion the fact that members of one set can be members of a different set.

10. Who would like to be a leader and give the class a set of movement challenges? List out loud a set of challenges for the class. When you are done say, "Go!" The class will perform the challenges in order and then make the shape of the number of challenges in the set. Can the leader give a set of challenges using level?

The leader might say: "Walk on a low level"; "Skip on a high level"; "Push on a medium level"; "Go!" The class then tries to perform the challenges in order and makes the shape of the number three. Pick a new leader who might give a set of directional challenges. Besides providing practice with sets, this is a good exercise in listening, memory, and counting.

11. Each of you find a set of people in this classroom. For instance, everyone wearing tennis shoes could form a set. After you have found your set, think of some way for your set to move. We will go around the room, and each person will name his or her set and give them a movement challenge. All members of the set will perform the movement. I will go first. All the people wearing white socks stand up and hop three times to the right. Does everyone moving belong in the set? Is there anyone not moving who should be in the set? Let's go on.

12. *(This problem introduces subsets.)* Each person in the class

think of a fruit that you would like to describe through movement. *(Name many fruits so that there will be a wide variety of choices.)* Now, we have a big set of fruit. Let us try to make smaller sets from the big set. I will go first. I would like to see the set of yellow fruits move. Can you guess the fruits to be sure that everyone moving belongs in the set of yellow fruits? Who can think of another set?

Other sets might be red fruits, purple fruits, crunchy fruits, soft fruits, juicy fruits, fruits with pits, fruits with peels, fruits with skins, round fruits, or oval fruits. Try other categories of sets such as food, machines, plants, vehicles, and occupations.

13. A subset is a part of a set. We were using subsets in the problem about the different kinds of fruit. Let's work with numbers now. Look what I have written on the board: A = $\{1,2,3,4,5\}$, B = $\{2,4\}$. *B* is a subset of *A* because 2 and 4 are in both sets. An empty set and the set itself are subsets of every set. Can you list all the subsets of A = $\{1,2,3\}$? There are eight of them: $\{1\}$, $\{2\}$, $\{3\}$, $\{1,2\}$, $\{2,3\}$, $\{1,3\}$, $\{1,2,3\}$, $\{\quad\}$ (empty set).

Now, I am going to give each group a set of numbers. Find all the subsets of the set and make the numbers with your body. Think of some way to show the empty set. When every group is ready, we will look at the subsets of each set. *(Use sets such as: A = $\{6,7\}$; B = $\{1,3,5\}$; C = $\{31\}$; etc.)*

Variation: Use objects instead of numbers or elements of movement such as A = $\{$ twisted shape, curved shape, angular shape$\}$; B = $\{$ high level, low level$\}$; C = $\{$ run, hop, jump, walk$\}$. A set with four members will have fourteen subsets.

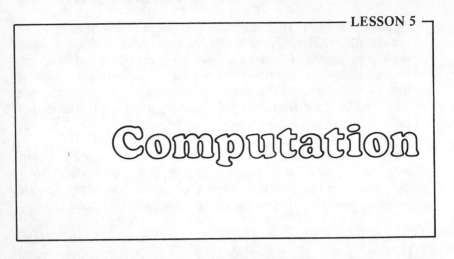

Computation

Any problems in your math books can be translated into movement problems by having students form the pictures, numbers, and signs with their bodies or body parts. Below are a few more ideas.

1. Who would like to help with an addition and subtraction problem? I would like one person to come to the front of the room and stand. How many people do you see standing? [One.] Another person come up and stand next to the first. How many people do you see now? [Two.] One person plus one person equals two people. Now one of you sit down. How many are left? Two people minus one person equals one person.

   If the children are able, have them draw or write what they see. Continue in this manner with other addition and subtraction problems.

2. Who would like to come up and make an interesting shape (or the shape of a specific object)? Now, I need two more people to come up and copy the first shape. Stand next to the first person. Who would like to be a plus sign? Now let us add two more shapes. Make your shapes look like the first shapes but stand a little apart from them, on the other side of the plus sign. Who would like to be an equal sign? How many shapes do you see altogether? Good, we need five more shapes to show the answer. Make your shapes look just like the first shape. Can the rest of you draw or write the problem you see on your paper?

Who can tell me what this equation says? The answer is 2 + 3 = 5. ("Computation," Problem 1)

Young children might draw the shapes, for example: △ △ △ + △ △ = △ △ △ △ △. *Older children might write 3 + 2 = 5. This is an excellent exercise in shape recognition along with practice in addition.*

(If the children are ready for subtraction, continue.) Who could rearrange these shapes to create a subtraction problem? Now write down the new problem that you see. Is there another way to write the problem? Who can move the shapes to show another subtraction problem? Keep the shapes in the same groupings. *(Solutions: 5 – 3 = 2, 5 – 2 = 3.)*

Ask the children to suggest numbers and shapes to use in problems. For instance, six circles plus three circles, or one dog plus four dogs.

3. Someone give me two numbers they would like to use in a problem. Who can come up and make the shape of those numbers? *(Choose as many students as you need to make the shapes of the two numbers.)* We also need a plus *(or multiplication)* sign and an equal sign. Now, who has figured out the

Is this equation correct? Does 1 + 7 = 8? ("Computation," Problem 3)

answer? Good. Can you come up and make the answer with your body? Bring a friend if you need help in making the number. Who can create a subtraction *(or division)* problem using these numbers? Come up and show the numbers where to move to display a new problem.

4. Let us make an equation with more than two addends *(or factors)*. Someone give me three numbers to use in our equation. Who can make the shape of the numbers? Now, let's group two numbers together in parentheses. Can I have two parentheses up here? What two numbers should we group together first? Parentheses, get around those two numbers. What is the sum *(or product)* of the two numbers? Who can make that number in front of the two numbers? Now we only have two addends *(or factors)* which makes it easier to find the answer. What is the answer? Everyone make the answer with their bodies. Now, what other two numbers could we put the parentheses around?

Repeat the above process until all the solutions have been discovered. With three addends (or factors) there are twelve possible solutions: (3 + 2) + 4; (3 + 4) + 2; 3 + (4 + 2); 3 + (2 + 4); (4 + 2) + 3; 4 + (3 + 2); 4 + (2 + 3); (4 + 3) + 2; (2 + 3) + 4; 2 + (3 + 4); (2 + 4) + 3; 2 + (4 + 3); or (3 x 4) x 2; 3 x (4 x 2), etc.

5. *This activity can be used after children have completed a page of vertical math problems like these:*

6	4	10	3	5	2
+8	+2	-4	+5	+9	x7
14	6	6	8	14	14

Do not mix operations if the children are not ready.

Let's look at the first line of answers. We will read the answers together out loud, but every time your answer is 14, clap instead of saying it out loud.

The line above would be: clap, six, six, eight, clap, clap. Decide on other numbers to clap. This will produce different rhythms. Also try actions instead of sounds such as punch, arm lift, kick, stretch, bend, twist, etc.

6. Find a partner. One of you clap a certain number of times while you both count the claps. Then the other person will clap while you both count again. Finally the first person will clap the answer (depending on what mathematical operation is called for). Number one might clap seven times. Number two might clap three times. How many times will number one have to clap? [Number one should clap ten times for addition, twenty-one times for multiplication.] Take turns clapping first. Besides clapping, try other sounds or movements to add *(or multiply)* together.

This problem can also be used for practice with subtraction or division. Number one claps. Number two claps a smaller amount of claps and number one claps the answer. This problem also works well with trios. Number three claps the answer instead of number one.

7. *(Divide the class into groups.)* I am going to give each group an addition, subtraction, multiplication, or division problem. Form the problem in your group. When everyone is ready, we

Here student one bounces the ball; student two adds bounces; and
student three bounces the sum. ("Computation," Problem 6)

will look at each group and try to solve the problem. *(The
groups can then think of their own problems to challenge
other groups.)*

8. I am going to put even and odd problems on the board like
this: $E + O =$, $E + E =$, $O + O =$, $E - E =$, $E - O =$, $O - O =$, $O \times
O =$, $\square \times E = E$, $E \times O =$, $O \div O =$, $E \div O =$, $E \div E =$. If the
answer is even, make the letter E with your body. If the
answer is odd, make an O with your body. *(Instead of letters,
you might ask for actions using levels, directions, force,
tempo, etc.)*

9. *For this activity, you need a spinner with nine numbers on it
(1-9 or those of your choosing). You also need a heavy piece
of cardboard, 3-feet square, and divided into nine sections.
Each section should contain one of the nine numbers shown
on the spinner—in any order. (See Diagram 7.)*

Choose someone in your group or pair to spin the numbers.

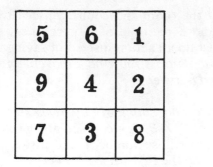

Diagram 7. ("Computation," Problem 9)

Put one body part on the first number spun, a second part on the second number, and then say the sum of the numbers *(or the remainder, product, or quotient.)* If you are correct, you can be the next spinner.

With older children, ask them to put as many body parts as possible on the board and still keep their balance, like the game "Twister." When they cannot move, they add their numbers.

10. *Give each student a number (sum, difference, or product) depending on whether you want to reinforce addition, subtraction, or multiplication skills. If adding, start with 5 and run consecutively as far as needed. If subtracting, start with 1. If multiplying, use products such as 4, 8, 12, 16, 20, etc.*

The first person to start taps his knees, claps his hands, snaps right fingers and calls out a number, and snaps left fingers and calls out a number. The person whose number is the sum *(difference or product)* of those two numbers picks up the rhythm and gives two new numbers. Who can play without missing a beat? Let's try.

The game might go: tap, clap, snap 2, snap 4. Then number 6 would tap, clap, snap 8, snap 7, and number 15 would pick up the rhythm. For subtraction, make the rule: Call out the larger number first. For multiplication, you might ask that only even or odd numbers be used depending on the products given out. Instead of snapping, try punching, turning, swaying, pushing, pulling, etc.

11. We are going to go around the room and count consecutively starting with 1. Every time a multiple of 7 is reached, the person whose turn it is must do an action instead of saying the number. *(Variation: The whole class must do a movement for every multiple of the chosen number.)*

12. *(Have children form a circle and count off by fives starting with five, i.e. 5, 6, 7, 8, 9; 5, 6, 7, 8, 9, etc.)* I am going to call out math problems. Everyone whose number is the answer run around the circle and try to be the first person home.

You can also play this game as a circle relay race with two teams racing against each other. Give two points to the first one home and one point to the second one home so that everybody gets at least one point. Use higher numbers and multiples for the older children. Occasionally, call out two problems. The game will run smoothly if you think of problems ahead of time and put them on cards for yourself. Try problems such as: 3 + 4 − 2; 2 x 5 − 1 x 3; 16 ÷ 8 + 4; or simpler ones depending on the students' level.

13. *Draw a large tic-tac-toe board on paper or on the playground and write numbers in the squares. (See Diagram 8.) Divide the children into two teams of six each. If you wish, this problem could be used to introduce children to number lines. The teams could keep score by using markers to indicate cumulative scores along a number line.*

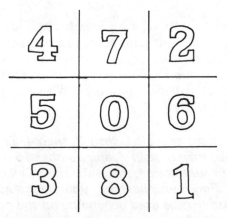

Diagram 8. ("Computation," Problem 13)

We are going to play "Body Tic-Tac-Toe." The first person to start picks a spot on the board to stand on. Make an interesting shape or the shape of the number you are standing on. Now someone on the other team pick a square to stand on. Keep alternating until one team has three squares in a row. Now the winning team add up the numbers in the three squares. That is your score. Mark the score on your number line. Play another game. The losing team gets to start first. Keep your scores on your number line. Stop playing when one team reaches 30 (or any predetermined total).

Variations: (a) If the game is played with partners, have each individual put a body part in a square until someone has three body parts in a row. (b) Have students answer math problems, such as 8 x 9 = ?, before they can pick spaces on the board.

14. *(Divide the class into groups.)* Think of an equation in your group, and find as many different ways to form that equation as possible. We will look at all the solutions and see which group came up with the most solutions.

    Some examples: 2 + 3 = 5; 3 + 2 = 5; $+\frac{3}{5}2$; II + III = V; (II) +

    (III) = (IIIII); 5 = 2 + 3; 5 = 3 + 2; $+\frac{2}{5}3$; III + II = V; (III) + (II)

    = (IIIII); two + three = five (make letters with body shapes).

15. Someone pick a number. How many mathematical problems can you think of that result in that number?

    This activity should be an ongoing one as the solutions are almost endless. Children might write the problems on a roll of butcher paper as they think of them and form the new equations with their bodies before the daily math lesson. The variety and number of solutions will depend on the grade level of the children. This is a very motivating and exciting activity.

16. Let's play "Who Am I?" I will ask a mathematical question out loud *(or write it on the board)* and you show me the answer with a body shape.

Some examples: I am 1 more than 5; I am 3 less than 8 and 4; I am less than 6, greater than 2 and even; I am 4 tens and five tens; I am ¼ of 2 and 4, etc.

17. This is a game of "True and False." I am going to write a mathematical sentence on the board. If it is true, make a shape on a high level. If it is false, make a shape on a low level.

    Try other actions such as push-pull, twist-turn, fast-slow, forward-backward, right-left, strong-weak, walk-run, etc. Some examples are: 52 + 5 = 59, 8 + 2 = 10, 3 + 4 + 6 = 14, (6 − 5) + 3 = 8, 15 ÷ 3 = 5, ½ of (3 + 5 + 12) = 10, 2 + 6 + 8 < 5 + 3 + 4, etc.

18. Let's make a factor triangle. Do you think we can find the prime factors for the number 72 and make the factors with body shapes? We should end up with a big triangle of factors. We need two people to form 72. Now, what are two factors of 72? Good. We need a 6 and a 12. *(Also an x sign if there are enough people.)* What are the factors of 6? of 12? Now, there is one more number to be made into factors. Good. We should have 12 numbers altogether. I am going to divide the class in half and give each half the same number. Which half can find and form all the factors the fastest?

    The end shape for 72 should look like this:

    72
    6 x 12
    2 x 3 x 4 x 3
    2 x 3 x 2 x 2 x 3

19. *In this problem the students divide into groups and form a human number wheel. See Diagram 9 for an example of an addition number wheel formation.*

    Can your group make a human number wheel? Choose someone to make the shape of a number and pick an operation (addition, subtraction, etc.). Now several more of you form a small circle around the center number and make number shapes. Those left form a bigger circle, each standing next to one of the numbers. Now, find the answer by (adding,

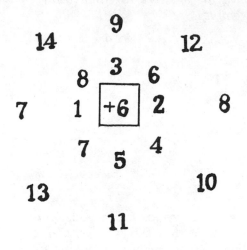

Diagram 9. An addition number wheel formation. ("Computation," Problem 19)

subtracting, etc.) the center number and the one you are standing near. Make the shape of the answer with your body.

Variations: (a) Have one group make just the inside circle, and ask other groups to form the answer. (b) After forming one answer, the outside wheel moves one person to the right. The inside circle has to form the reverse operation to find the number that would complete the new equation. They make the new number and the outside wheel moves again to repeat the process. (c) The inside wheel moves to the right, and the outside numbers have to find and form the answer for the new equation. (d) The two wheels move in opposite directions until the center number says "Stop." Then either outside or inside numbers have to change to form a correct equation. Determine ahead of time who will change. Repeat several times. (e) A number card is placed in the center instead of a person. This allows everyone to practice computation.

20. *(Divide the class into groups or use the whole class when necessary.)* I am going to put an equation on the board. Can your group form an array for each equation?

   You may want to write problems without answers and have

the groups give the answers for their arrays. Here are some interesting examples:

a. 1 x 6 = 6 ......   *c. 4 x 3 = 12 ...*
                                              . . .
b. 3 x 4 = 12 ....   *. . .*
      . . . .   *. . .*
      . . . .

d. (4 x 2) + (4 x 3) = 20 ..   ... (2 groups slightly apart)
                              . .   . . .
                              . .   . . .
                              . .   . . .

21. *(Divide the class into groups.)* Can your group make an array for which the rest of the class will write an equation? Instead of just standing still, try making a moving array. Use different shapes, nonlocomotor movement, speeds, and force. Could your whole array move through general space? Try it.

22. *(Use groups for this problem.)* I am going to give you some short story problems to solve through movement. First, make the shape of the objects or act out the story; then form an equation to represent your story.

Use story problems from your math text or have the children make up their own. Here is an example and some possible solutions:

   Problem: John had 3 apples, Mary had 4. Mary gave 2 apples to John. How many apples did she have left?

Solutions: (a) Three children make apple shapes on one side of the room and 4 children make apple shapes on the other side of the room. Two apples from the 4-apple set then roll over to the 3-apple set. (b) A boy picks 3 children to be apples near him, and a girl picks 4 children to be apples near her. Then the girl leads 2 children over to the boy and goes back to her remaining 2 apples.

Some of the story problems can be very funny. For example: 4 monsters, 5 noses on each monster. How many noses altogether? As the solution, 4 children could form 5 noses on their faces using fingers and dance around like monsters. Meanwhile, the remaining children count the noses to come up with the answer. The monsters then form the correct equation with body shapes: 4 x 5 = 20 or 5 + 5 + 5 + 5 = 20.

23. *Divide the class into small groups. Make a duplicate set of cards for each group with problems written on them such as: (a) Move at a low level to the (4 – 2) + 2 desk in the (8 + 5) – 9 row; (b) walk backwards to the (5 x 2) – (3 + 4) shelf of the bookcase; and (c) crawl to the (9 ÷ 3) + 0 window.*

I am going to give each group a task card. When your group has successfully completed the task on the card, I will give you another card. When your group has gone through the deck of cards, sit down at your seats.

Children enjoy making up similar task cards for each other.

24. *(Divide the class into groups.)* Can your group show me with body numbers, shapes, or letters an example of the associative principle? [a + (b + c) = (a + b) + c, a x (b x c) = (a x b) x c] Can you show me the commutative principle? [a + b = b + a, a x b = b x a] Can you show me an example of the distributive principle? [a x (b + c) = (a x b) + (a x c)]

25. Pick one of the mathematical principles we have been studying, and using body numbers, create a problem that uses that principle. When your group is ready, the rest of us will guess the principle and work out the problem.

The following problems use number lines. One or more large number lines can be drawn on the floor or playground with chalk, paint, or tape (make long cross lines if working in groups). Large, vinyl, walk-on number lines can be ordered from school-supply companies.

26. I am going to clap a certain number of times as you jump forward on the number line. Each time I clap, jump one number. Then I will pause as you look at the number you landed on. I will clap a few more times. Count the second group of claps in your head, starting with *1* as you jump. When I stop, look at the number you landed on. Can you tell me the

two numbers of claps that you jumped? Good. Now add the
two numbers together. What is the answer?

*For example: Clap four times, and the child lands on 4. Clap
three more times as the child counts "1, 2, 3" and lands on 7
(4 + 3 = 7). Reverse the process for subtraction, having the
children jump toward 0. The other children can clap with you
if you hold up fingers to represent the number you want
clapped.*

27. Start on *0* on the number line. I will give commands to follow
such as "Hop three *2s*," "Walk two *6s*," or "Crawl five *3s*."
When you land on the answer, make the shape of the number
you landed on.

*Encourage the children to count "one 2, two 2s, three 2s" as
they move so they can keep track of their sets of numbers.*

*Variations: (a) Use addition problems such as "Skip 3 + 4"
or "Leap 8 + 2." (b) Use a "Simon Says" or "Mother May I"
format for the commands.*

Measurement

Time

1. Let us pretend we are clocks. Clocks mark time in three ways. Can you name the three ways? [Seconds, minutes, hours.] Show me a clock that is just marking seconds. How would that clock move? You can move your whole body or body parts. *(Possible solutions are: running, arms or legs making fast circles, rocking quickly back and forth, etc.)* How would a clock move that is just marking the hours? Show me. *(Possible solutions: giant steps, slow arm or leg circles with starts and stops, slow rocking.)* Now, show me how a clock marking the minutes would look. How was each clock different? [The second clock had a fast tempo; the hour clock, a slow tempo; and the minute clock, a medium tempo.]

2. I am going to divide you into six groups. The first two groups mark seconds through movement. The second two groups mark minutes, and the third two groups mark hours. Work as individuals in the groups, doing any movement you feel fits best with your clock. Everybody practice.

Now, let's watch one of the first two groups, one of the second two, and one of the third two. We will see the seconds, minutes, and hours all working together. Now, let's watch the other half of each group perform. Could you tell the seconds, minutes, and hours apart? How? [They were moving at different tempos.]

3. *(Divide the class into three groups: seconds, minutes, hours.)*

121

We can be more precise if we use musical accompaniment *(or a metronome)*. I will play eighth notes for the seconds; quarter notes, which are half as slow, for the minutes; and half notes, which are half again as slow, for the hours. When I clap *(or beat on the drum)* eighth notes, the group of seconds will move. When I clap quarter notes, the minutes will move, and when I clap half notes, the hours will move. Listen for your tempo. When you hear it, move in any way you wish but keep in time with the music.

Clap alternating half, quarter, and eighth notes. This activity also gives practice in tempo, a measurement of music.

4. Find two friends to work with. You will be working together to form a clock. One will be the hour hand, one the minute hand, and one the second hand. Think of an interesting

Can you demonstrate the speed of the second, minute, and hour hands on a clock? The children in the foreground are the minute hands; the children in the center are the second hands; and the children in the back row are the hour hands. ("Measurement: Time," Problem 4)

formation and movements to describe your clock. Are you going to be an alarm clock, a cuckoo clock, a grandfather clock, a digital clock, a watch? Remember you will each be moving at a different speed. When everyone is ready, we will look at all the different clocks.

5. Who would like to stand up and be a clock? Show the class 4:00 using your arms and legs. Can you make one body part shorter than the other so that we can tell the hour hand from the minute hand? Who can show us 3:00? 5:00? 7:45?

Variations: (a) Have each child think of a time to show. The students then guess each other's times. (b) Divide the children into groups. Have each group make a large clock. Give problems on time to each group or have groups give problems to each other.

6. *Read poems, riddles, or stories that deal with time. Have the children act out the story and make clock faces or numbers at*

Can you make a clock that says 9:00? ("Measurement: Time," Problem 5)

the appropriate places. Ask the children to make up stories, riddles, or rhymes about time to act out. Some examples of riddles follow:

It's twelve fifty-five;　　　　　　Right now it's ten o'clock
School starts at one.　　　　　　The movie starts at three.
I have only＿＿＿＿＿;　　　　　　I'm going to have＿＿＿＿＿;
I'm going to have to run.　　　　That's time to trim the tree.

At seven o'clock it's out of bed; I stretch my arms and legs.
At eight o'clock it's breakfast time; I feel like toast and eggs.
At nine o'clock I run to school; I want to be on time.
At ten o'clock we work on math; I'm feeling very fine.
At eleven o'clock we go to music; and there we sing a song.
At twelve o'clock it's home for lunch; I won't be hungry long.

7. *(Put a calendar on the board.)* Answer my questions by making letter shapes or number shapes. What day of the week was September 25th? What day of the week was September 29th? How many days are in-between? What is the date before

Make a famous date in history with number shapes. This group is forming 1776. ("Measurement: Time," Problem 10)

the 6th? after the 6th? How many days were in the whole month? How many days were in the first week? the last week? How many Mondays were there? How many Saturdays were there? *(Continue with other questions. Compare other months.)*

8. Can you make the number shape of the month you were born in? the day you were born on? the year you were born in?

9. If the year was 1982 and you were born in 1961, how old would you be? Make your age in number shapes. *(Continue with similar problems.)*

10. *(Divide the class into small groups.)* Each group think of a famous date or holiday. Make the date with number shapes. The rest of us will try to guess the date and tell why it is famous. Can you make a second date on a different level?

11. Can you answer my questions by making number shapes? How many days in September? April? June? and November? All the rest have ____, except February which has ____. But every how many years is one day added ____, to give February ____? *(Keep repeating the jingle until the children can say it as they make number shapes.)*

Linear

1. Can you measure the room in giant steps? How many giant steps does it take you to go from one end to the other? Now, from one side to the other? Try going around all four sides of the room. Now measure the room in baby steps, heel to toe. How did your measurements change?

2. Find something to measure in hands. Hands are still used to measure horses. How many hands high (fingers spread out) is your desk? your friend? the bookcase? your paper?

3. Let's measure the room in people. How many people lying down head to toe can fit in our room? How wide is the room in people standing arms-width apart? Do you think we would get the same number if we used adults instead of children? Why?

4. Measure the length of your desk with as many different body parts as you can think of. How many knees is it? How many forearms is it? Write down your measurements for each body part. We will compare body parts and measurements. *(Continue, measuring other objects.)*

5. Show me through movement what *height* means; what *length* means; *width; perimeter; circumference; diameter.*

    Use only the vocabulary familiar to the children. They will come up with many interesting solutions if you encourage them to keep thinking of new ways to move using the elements of movement.

6. Answer my questions with number shapes. How many inches in a foot? How many feet in a yard? How many inches in a yard? How many feet in two yards?

    Continue with similar questions going into perimeter, diameter, etc. if the children are studying those areas.

Weight

1. I am going to hold up two pictures. Make the shape of the object that you think weighs the most. *(After showing several pictures, ask for the object that weighs the least. Start with simple comparisons such as an elephant and a feather. Work up to more difficult ones such as an elephant and a horse.)*

2. Pretend you are picking up a heavy, heavy rock. What does your body do? What happens to your muscles? [They become tight or tense.] Are all your body parts working of just a few? [All body parts should work. The more body parts you use, the greater force you create.] Are your body parts close together or apart? [They should be apart. The greater the range of motion, the more force is created.]

    Now pretend you are picking up a scrap of paper. *(Repeat the above questions. The answers are just the opposite: Muscles are relaxed; few body parts are working; and body parts are closer together.)*

Let's try some other pretend objects. The class will try to guess how much your object weighs (in general terms) by the shape and tension of your muscles. Try many different shapes and levels. Can you move through space with your imaginary object?

3. Can you use different body parts to hold your weight? Usually your legs hold your weight. Could your back hold your weight? your stomach? arms and legs? arms and legs in a different way? one arm and one leg? knees? buttocks? toes? hands? head and hands?

   You may not want to do head- and handstands unless adequate facilities such as open space and mats are available. Ask the children for more body part combinations that can hold their weight.

   When was it hardest to hold your weight? [When small or weak body parts were used.] Can you hold your weight on different body parts and move through space? Try moving your weight shapes in different directions with changes in speed.

   With younger children, the use of animal imagery is helpful in getting them into shapes and moving through space. Use animals such as snake (stomach), dinosaur (hands and feet), crab (hands and feet—stomach up), and whale on back (back).

4. Can you hold someone else's weight? Stand back to back. One of you lunge forward so that your back is on a slant. The other person relax and let your friend hold your weight. You should feel as though you were leaning against a slanted board. Now the lunging partner straighten up slowly, and the leaning partner lunge forward slowly. Keep your backs glued together and feel the moment of weight shift. Is there a moment when neither of you are holding weight? [When both are standing straight up.]

   Can you do this activity standing side by side? Now you will carry your partner's weight on your side instead of your back. Is it easier to hold the weight as you go down or as you straighten up? Why? [It is easier going down because of gravity

Can you hold someone else's weight? Here one child is lunging forward, slanting her back, while the other child leans and relaxes against her. ("Measurement: Weight," Problem 4)

pulling on the object. Therefore, it is easier to lay down a heavy object than it is to pick one up.]

5. How would you move if you weighed five hundred pounds? Show me using directions, levels, pathways, and speed. Could you jump, skip, hop, or leap? How would you do those movements if you could? Do you get very far off the ground? Why? Now, show me how a very thin person moves. What was different about your thin person movements compared to your fat person movements?

If you have overweight children in your classroom, you may not want to do this activity.

6. Show me with number shapes the answers to these questions. How many ounces in a pound? How many pounds in a ton?

How many ounces in a ton? How many ounces in two pounds? in four pounds? in one and one-half pounds? *(Continue with similar questions geared toward your grade level.)*

7. Show me with letter shapes the abbreviation for ounce; for pound; for ton.

8. I'm going to give you riddles. Answer the riddle by making the shape of the answer with your body.
   a. Which weighs more: a pound of feathers or six ounces of rocks? [feathers]
   b. Which weighs the least: seventeen ounces of sugar cubes or one pound of cookies? [cookies]
   c. Which weighs the most: one and one-half pounds of pencils or twenty ounces of erasers? [pencils]
   d. Which weighs the least: one ton of bricks or two thousand pounds of clouds? [Both weigh the same.]

Ask the children to make up riddles for each other. Give all the children a chance to figure out and make the shape of the answer. You may do this in a circle with all the children facing out so they cannot see each other. The riddle-maker stands in the middle and makes the shape of the answer. At a signal, the others turn around and check their answers with the riddle-maker's.

Volume

1. *Use the following problems in "Measurement: Weight": Problem 1, substituting the word "holds" for "weighs," and Problems 6, 7, and 8, using the terms "cups," "pints," "quarts," and "gallons" instead of the units of weight.*

2. *(Divide the class into groups.)* Can half of your group make the shape of a gallon container? Use any level you wish. Now fill the container with two quarts of people. How much of the container should be filled? [One-half.] Now fill your gallon container with four cups of people. How much of your container is filled with people? [One-quarter.] Try making a quart container on a different level. Fill your container with four cups of people. How much of your container is filled? [The whole container.] Find different ways to make con-

Can you fill a quart container with two cups of people? ("Measurement: Volume," Problem 2)

tainers and different ways to fill your container with people as I ask you more questions.

Have groups watch other groups and make up problems for them to solve. This activity provides work with fractions along with volume.

3. *(Divide the class into groups.)* In your group make the shape of a sphere and fill in one-half the volume with people. Remember that a sphere is three-dimensional. Can you make a cube and fill in one-fourth of the volume? Try a cylinder and fill in two-thirds of the volume. Can you show me a pyramid with all the volume filled? Try a cone and fill in as much volume as you wish. We will try to guess the amount filled in. *This activity provides a good review of geometrical shapes and fractions.*

Money

1. Can you answer my questions by making number shapes? How many cents in a penny? in a nickel? in a dime? in a quarter? in a half-dollar? in a dollar? *(Use only the money units you have studied.)*

2. Can you answer my questions with letter shapes? With what letter does another word for one cent begin? for five cents? for ten cents? for twenty-five cents? for fifty cents? for one hundred cents?

3. Can you make the shape of the cents sign (¢) with your body? Try the dollar sign ($). Try the signs on different levels and with other body parts.

4. I am going to hold up a picture of apples. If each apple cost five cents, how much money would you need to buy all the apples? Show me with your body. Remember to make the right sign so I will know if you are talking about cents or dollars. *(Continue with other pictures and questions.)*

5. Let's play store. I'll be the shopper and each of you will be a clerk. Instead of giving me real money for change, can you clap out the number of cents you owe me? Let's try. This pencil costs fifteen cents. I only have a quarter. How much change should I get? Ready, clap. This eraser costs five cents. I give you a nickel. How much change should I get? Ready, clap. *(There should be silence.)* This book costs three dollars and ninety-eight cents. I will give you four dollars. How much money do you owe me? Ready, clap.

   Continue with similar problems. You may ask the class to respond as a group or as individuals. Partners enjoy working together during free time.

6. Let's think of a sound or movement for each coin. *(Perhaps clap for a penny, stamp for a nickel, snap for a dime, punch for a quarter, knock for a half-dollar, and turn for a dollar. Solicit other ideas from the children.)*

   I will write a price tag on the board and ask you to repeat it using our new code for coins. If the price tag is $2.35, you

Which costs more: a toy boat for three nickels or a pencil for fourteen pennies? These children are indicating their answers by making boat shapes. ("Measurement: Money," Problem 7)

would make two turns, three snaps, and a stamp. Are you ready? Let's try a few together, and then I will ask for individual volunteers.

You may also use this activity for making change as in Problem 5. For the younger children, write the list of sounds and actions next to pictures of the corresponding coins on the chalkboard. Write simple price tags such as 4¢, 5¢, 10¢, 12¢, 15¢, etc. This activity provides a good review for place value and counting.

7. I am going to put two pictures on the board and write the price under each item. Make the shape of the item in the picture that costs the most.

    Instead of pictures you could write the item and price on the board: pencil—10¢, eraser—9¢, book—$2.40, meat—$2.50.

Fractions

1. Can you make one-half of your body stretch? Can you make one-half of your body bend? Can you find another way to divide your body in half? [Right and left, up and down.] Now can you make one-half bend while the other half stretches? Try dividing your body in another way and doing that. Can you make strong muscles on one-half of your body? weak muscles on one-half? push with one-half? pull with one-half? move quickly with one-half? move slowly with one-half? *(Continue with other actions.)*

2. Let's divide the body into thirds: armpits on up is one-third, armpits to hips is another third, and hips to toes is the last third. Can you bend one-third of your body? twist one-third? stretch one-third? Can you do all those movements at one time with each third? Can you put all your body parts in one-third of your self space? in two-thirds of your self space? in three-

Can one-half of your body bend while the other half stays straight? Each of these children have a different solution. ("Measurement: Fractions," Problem 1)

thirds of your self space? Is there any way to put body parts in the top third and the bottom third and not in the middle third? [No.] Can you put body parts in the upper two-thirds of your space and not in the bottom? [Yes, by sitting on a chair, table, ladder, etc.]

Besides working on thirds, this activity is excellent for developing coordination. Ask for other challenges from the children.

3. Can you run one-half of the distance of the room? skip one-half? jump? hop? leap? crawl? gallop? slide? Can you walk one-third of the distance of the room? skip? roll? Can you leap one-fourth of the distance of the room? *(Continue with other fractions and other movements using level, direction, force, and speed.)*

4. *(Hold up pictures, like those in Diagram 10, to illustrate your questions.)* Answer my questions by making the correct fraction with your body. Make the shape of the numerator first and the denominator second. What part of the squares is colored blue? What part of the triangles is colored red? What part of the circles is colored green? *(Continue with similar problems.)*

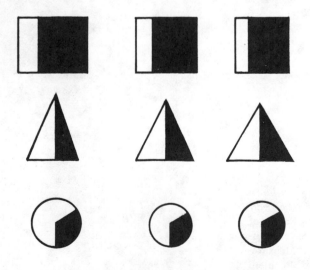

Diagram 10. ("Measurement: Fractions," Problem 4)

5. *(Divide the class into groups.)* Can your group make a rectangle and fill in one-fourth of it? *(It is easier to do this lying down, or a rectangle could be drawn on the floor instead of using bodies to form one.)* Can you fill in one-third of the rectangle? Now, pick a fraction of the rectangle to fill in and we will guess each group's fraction.

6. *(Divide the class into groups.)* Make an interesting geometrical shape. Then form a line with your bodies that will cut the shape into two equal parts. Try another shape on a different level. Try another shape, and we will look at the different shapes to see if the two parts are equal.

7. Answer these questions by hopping the correct number of times: 1/3 of 15 is? 1/4 of 8 is? 2/3 of 18 is? 1/2 of 14 is? *(Instead of hopping, use other locomotor or nonlocomotor movements.)*

Music: Volume, Pitch, and Tempo

Volume

1. I am going to beat on the drum. Some beats will be louder than others. When you hear loud beats, make big, forceful movements. When you hear soft beats, make small, light movements. To let you get ready, I will play a few beats of different volume before you move.

   Play a few beats; then give the signal to move. The first time you do this activity, make the difference between the loud beats and soft beats very distinct. As time goes on, bring the volumes closer together so that it is more difficult to distinguish between loud and soft.

2. Can you move softly when you hear the loud beats *(or music)* and loudly when you hear the soft beats? *(After some practice, continue.)* Was that hard to do? Why? *(It is often hard for children to move against the music.)* Let's try it again, and this time include different levels and directions in your movement.

3. *(This activity uses rhythm band instruments.)* Let's divide the

Change your movements each time the volume of the orchestra changes.
As the orchestra plays loudly, the dancers' movements match the
music. ("Measurement: Music," Problem 3)

class in half. One-half will play while the other half moves.
Each half choose a conductor and decide on signals for loud
and soft. The conductor of the group will signal the orchestra
when to play loudly and when to play softly. The other group
will move to the music, changing their movements each time
the volume of the orchestra changes. After one group has
played, the other group will have a chance to be the orchestra.

Pitch

4. I am going to play notes on the piano. *(Or use a brass or
   woodwind instrument. A drum does not work.)* Some notes
   will be high on the scale, and some notes will be low. Can you
   make high level shapes when you hear high-pitched notes and
   low level shapes when you hear low-pitched notes? *(Bring the
   ranges closer together as the children have more practice.)*
   I'm going to play more notes. This time move your shapes
   through space with different force and on different pathways.

5. I am going to play one note on the piano. Listen carefully to it. Then I will play a second note. If the second note is higher than the first note, make a high level shape; if it is lower, make a low level shape. Then I will play a third note. Compare it to the second note and make a high or low shape. I will play about six notes altogether. Keep comparing the new note to the last one you heard.

Variation: With older children, let them try to match the degree of difference in pitch with the degree of difference in their body level. If the pitch is much *higher, their shapes should be very high. If the pitch is just a* little *lower their shapes should be just a little lower than their previous shapes.*

6. I am going to play music with high-pitched notes and music with low-pitched notes. Listen to each piece and move the way the music makes you feel. When both pieces are over, we will discuss your movements.

Play each piece of music for about one minute. Then ask questions such as: How did you move with the high-pitched music? What level were you on? What locomotor movements did you do? What nonlocomotor movements did you do? Did the music make you move a certain way? Ask similar questions about the low-pitched music. Make sure all the children are talking about the same piece of music.

Tempo

7. I am going to beat *(or play)* two series of notes. Just listen to the music. When I am through, make a quick movement if the second series was faster than the first. Make a slow movement if the second series was slower than the first. *(Repeat the activity several times varying the tempo.)*

8. Can you quickly form three even lines? *(Or as many lines as you wish. Shorter lines insure everyone getting a chance to be leader.)* The first person in line will be the first leader. Follow your leader around the room copying his or her movements and *tempo.* The leader must keep the same tempo as long as he or she is leading. When I beat the drum once, the leader will run to the end of the line, and the next person will become the

leader. They new leader has to change the tempo. You cannot do the same two tempos in a row. Each time I beat the drum, change leaders. Try to do interesting movements while moving at different tempos.

Rhythm band instruments may be used. The children play their instruments to keep time with their movements.

9. I am going to play a record at three different speeds. *(Use an old record and play the same piece at 33-1/3, 78, and 16.)* Listen to the music and try to match your movements to the tempo. When you think the music is fast, say "fast" as you are moving. Say "slow" for the music that is slow and say "medium" for the music that is not too slow or too fast.

Problem 10 integrates volume, pitch, *and* tempo.

10. I am going to play several short pieces of music for you. Move the way the music makes you feel. Listen to the volume, pitch, and tempo. Think of how they are affecting you. We will discuss the music and your movements and feelings after I have played all the pieces.

Play four to six very different pieces of music for about 30 to 40 seconds. Use pieces with high pitch and fast tempo; low pitch, loud volume, and slow tempo; low pitch, soft volume, and fast tempo; high pitch, slow tempo, and loud volume, etc. You can regulate the tempo and volume on the record player if you have trouble finding a variety of pieces.

Before we discuss the music, I am going to play a little bit from each piece to refresh your memory. How did this piece make you feel? How did the pitch, volume, and tempo affect your movement? What movements did you do? What were you thinking of as you moved? *(Ask similar questions for the other pieces, then continue with more general questions.)* What kind of music would you like to hear in the dentist's office? Use the words pitch, volume, and tempo when describing it. What do you like to hear when you are sad? when you are happy? when you are scared?

Some children like to hear music that changes their moods, others like to hear music that complements their moods. Discuss this difference. You may want to draw the conclusion that although music affects each of us differently, it does affect our feelings and moods.

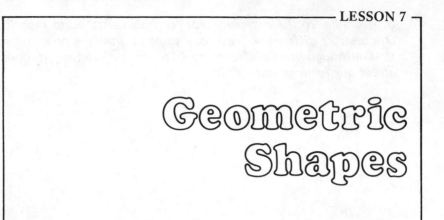

Geometric Shapes

1. Can you make the shape of a circle with your arms? with your legs? with your hands? with an arm and a leg? with your whole body? *(Repeat, using other geometric shapes and other body parts.)*

2. Look at the circle on the chalkboard. Can you draw the circle on the floor with your feet? Can you draw it in the air using your elbow? Can you draw it with your head? *(Repeat, using other shapes and other body parts as the pencil.)*

3. Can you walk in a circle? in a square? in a triangle? in a hexagon *(etc.)*? Can you hop in a circle? skip? gallop? slide? jump? *(Combine all the different locomotor movements with different shapes.)*

4. Can you walk backwards in a circle? in a square? Can you hop sideways in a triangle? Try jumping forwards in a rectangle. *(Combine locomotor movements, directions, and shapes. There are many, many combinations.)*

5. How many geometric shapes can you make with your body on a high level? on a low level? on a medium level? Can you make all the shapes we have been learning on each level?

6. Now try walking on a low level in a circle, on a high level in a square, on a medium level in a triangle. *(Combine levels, shapes, and locomotor movements.)*

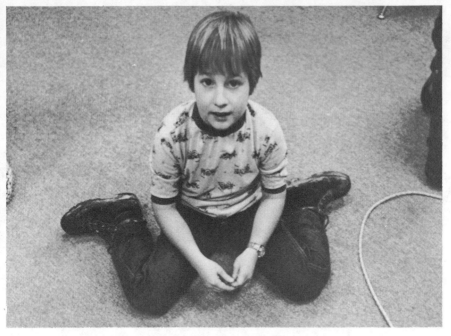

Can you make a triangle? ("Geometric Shapes," Problem 1)

Can you make a rectangle? ("Geometric Shapes," Problem 1)

Can you make a circle? ("Geometric Shapes," Problem 1)

7. Can you walk in a circle, and at the same time, make a circle with your body parts? *(Continue with other shapes.)*

8. Make the biggest triangle you can. Now make the smallest triangle, so tiny that I can hardly see it. Can you make a medium-sized triangle? *(The children are experiencing range of movement.)*

9. How many triangles can you make with your body at one time, using all your body parts? Let us look at each other and count all the triangles. Try some of your classmates' solutions. *(Substitute other shapes for triangle.)*

10. Make a big, strong circle shape with your body and freeze! When I give the signal, melt into a triangle and freeze. Melt into a rectangle and freeze.

Continue with other shapes. With the intermediate grades, add level. For example: Melt into a low-level triangle and freeze; melt into a high-level circle and freeze.

11. Find a partner. Trace a shape on your partner's back and have your partner guess the shape. Change places. Try all the different shapes you know.

12. Find a partner. Get behind your partner and steer him or her in a shape. Have your partner guess what shape you drew. Change places.

13. Let us play "Follow the Leader." The leader will lead the class around the room, drawing a big shape on the floor. When you guess the shape you are being led in, raise your hand and give the answer. The person who guesses the shape will be the new leader.

14. *For this problem, cut different geometric shapes—big enough for children to crawl through—out of the sides of a large box. If a box is not available, turn over furniture and tie string from piece to piece, forming geometric shapes.*

I'm going to give each person a different problem. When you are through, go to the end of the line. Here we go. Crawl in the circle and out the triangle. Crawl in the square and out the circle. Crawl in the rectangle and out the triangle.

Keep the children moving quickly so that no one is standing in line too long. To keep children busy while waiting in line, they could be tracing shapes on each other's backs. Both of these activities are excellent for perceptual-motor development.

15. Let us make a big circle. I'm going to pass out different cardboard shapes to each of you. There are triangles, squares, circles, and rectangles. *(Use more difficult shapes for older children.)* Each time I call out a shape, the people holding that shape stand up and run around the outside of the circle until they get back to their places. Then I will call out another shape.

You may add locomotor movement, direction, or level to this problem to make it more difficult. For example, if you call out "low triangle," those holding triangles would have to run around the circle on a low level. Other examples: backward circle, hopping squares, sideways rectangles, skipping octagons.

16. With a jump rope or a string, make a shape in front of you on the floor. Can you walk around the rope following its shape? Let us move around the room and try each other's shapes.

17. With your rope, make a shape on the floor in front of you. Can you turn your whole body into the shape of the rope? Lie down next to the rope and see if your body shape matches the rope shape. Try some of your friends' shapes. You can make the geometric shapes we have learned or crazy shapes you have made up.

Can you make a body shape that matches your rope shape? ("Geometric Shapes," Problem 17)

18. Let us make shape statues. In your groups, form interesting frozen statues using all the geometric shapes we have learned. Each person must be a different shape. Remember to use different levels and range to make your statue interesting. When you are done, we will show them to each other.

19. Make the shape of a triangle by yourself. Now, find a partner and make a triangle. Make a triangle with three people. Find another person and make a triangle with four people. Now make a triangle with five people. Can you make one with six people?

Try other shapes, and discuss which shapes are easiest with what number of people.

20. Get together with four or five friends and make a shape with all holding hands. Can you hop across the room and still keep your shape? You have to work together. Now drop your hands and hop across the room. This is harder. Try skipping; running; galloping; sliding; jumping; leaping.

21. I would like you to form two concentric circles. The inside circle will walk counterclockwise, and the outside circle will walk clockwise. Keep walking to the beat of the drum *(or music)*. You must keep the circles evenly spaced. The space between each person should be equal too. When I tap someone from the outside circle, that person will move to the inside circle, and everyone must adjust his or her space so it is even again. You will have to notice the space in front of you and behind you.

When there are only about five people left in the outside circle, begin to tap people in the inside circle to move back to the outside circle. Try other shapes besides the circle; they will be a challenge because of the angles.

22. Can you make a vibrating square? a swinging triangle? a sustained circle? a percussive hexagon?

Have the children try this alone and then in partners and small groups. Combine the different qualities of force with different shapes. Popular music creates a fun background for this activity.

23. *(Divide the class in half and thirds.)* Each group is going to make a shape obstacle course with their bodies for the other groups to move through. You can make circle bridges for climbing under or over, triangles for crawling through, circles on the floor like tires for jumping into, round bumps for jumping over, etc. Remember your course so that you can set it up again quickly after you have gone through the other ones.

Be sure to instruct the children to move carefully through the human obstacle course to avoid injuring other students.

24. Let us make one big shape all together. Walk around the room slowly. When I give the signal, see how quickly you can come together to make one big circle; one big square; a rectangle; a triangle; a pentagon. *(This activity takes a great deal of group cooperation and awareness.)*

25. Can you form objects just by putting different shapes together? I will divide you into groups and give each group a room in a house. Can you make an object or objects found in that room by putting triangles, squares, circles, etc. together? For example, if I gave you the dining room, you might make a table and chairs, china cabinet, or chandelier. We will try to guess your objects when you are ready.

You might also assign categories such as objects found in an office, a school room, on a farm, in the city, on the water, in the air, at the zoo.

26. How many objects can you think of that are round or have circles in them? Make the shape of a round object. Try to make your shape special in some way so that we can guess your object. For example, make a stem and some leaves at the top of your round apple shape. We will look at the shapes and make a list of the circular objects.

Some ideas are sun and planets, different kinds of balls, wheels, fruit, pottery, a frisbee, mirrors, etc. Continue this problem with square, rectangular, and triangular shaped objects.

PART III

SCIENCE PROBLEMS

PLANTS

Seasons

Animals

ELECTRICITY

MACHINES

Weather Planets

The Body

Heart

1. Can you find your pulse? Press your fingertips on the inside of your wrist. When you feel the beat of your pulse, tap out the rhythm with your foot. Now run in place as fast as you can. Take your pulse again and tap out the rhythm. What happened? [Pulse beat sped up.] What happens to your pulse when you are sleeping? [Slows down.] Take your pulse again. Is the rhythm even or uneven? [Even.] When you take your pulse you are listening to the beat of your heart. Your heart beats in a steady, even rhythm, but it can beat quickly, moderately, or slowly.

2. Take your pulse and tap out the rhythm with your foot. Once you have the tempo move in different ways and on different levels in your self space. Do one movement for each heartbeat. Now speed up your heartbeat by running in place. Find the rhythm and move through space at that tempo, jumping, hopping, leaping, and running in different directions. Now lie down and rest. Breathe slowly and let your heartbeat slow down. Listen to the slow rhythm and move slowly, making a different shape on each beat of your heart.

3. Make a big circle and sit down. Who would like to move around the circle in any way you wish? The rest of us will try to clap out your rhythm as you move around the circle and back to your home spot.

Have as many children move around the circle as time allows. Each child will move at a different tempo according to his or her internal rhythm. If you have rhythm band instruments, let the children accompany with them.

Lungs

4. Take a big breath and then let all the air out. How did your body move? Your chest expanded because your lungs filled with air. Then your chest collapsed because the air went out of your lungs. Your lungs are like two balloons. Take another deep, deep breath and let your arms lift up as your chest expands. Hold your breath and shape. Now let the air out and let your arms sink to the floor.

This time let your whole body lift up off the floor as you take a deep breath. Then sink back to the floor. Try taking short breaths as you expand your lungs and your shape. Every time you hold your breath, hold your shape. Now let the air out in short breaths as you sink to the floor. Every time you let your breath out, change your shape.

5. Can you create movement based on your breath? Take long breaths and short breaths and let your movement follow your breaths. Try many shapes, levels, and directions. Let each new breath start a new movement. We will divide the class in half and look at the breath phrases.

6. Pretend you are a balloon. Fill your lungs with air. Make a huge balloon shape with your body. Float all around the room. Watch out! There is a big hole in your balloon. What will happen? Put a patch on your balloon and fill it with air again. Float through general space, moving on different levels and in different directions. This time your balloon has a tiny leak in it. What happens to your balloon? How did your movement change with each break in the balloon? [Air rushed out the first time, and the human balloons deflated very quickly. The air leaked out slowly the second time, causing the human balloons to deflate slowly.]

What can we learn from this experiment about lungs and breath? [We can let the air out of our lungs in a big breath, or we can let the air out slowly, just as it leaked out of the balloon. In short, we can control our breathing.]

7. The heartbeat is an even continuous rhythm that we cannot stop at will. Is our breath the same way? [No; there is an uneven rhythm to breathing and breath can be held at will.] Find a partner. One of you create a heartbeat phrase and the other create a breath phrase. One of you should move in an even, machine-like rhythm, and the other should move in an uneven, airy rhythm. Who is the heart and who is the lung? We will guess when everyone is ready.

8. *(Divide the class into groups.)* Can each group create the heart and lungs? Where is the heart in relation to the lungs? How does the heart move compared to the lungs? How does the shape of the heart differ from the lungs? Answer all these questions through movement. We will watch each group when everyone is ready.

Bones

9. Can you rattle the bones in your body? Try not to use any muscles; just shake all your bones loosely in your self space. Shake just your hand bones; your arm bones; your feet bones; your leg bones; your back and rib bones; your neck and head bones.

10. What is the place called where two bones move against each other? [A joint.] How many ways can you move at your wrist joint? [Four: right, left, up, and down.] How many ways can you move at the elbow? [One.] How many ways can you move at the shoulder? [Around in a circle; the shoulder is a ball joint.] How many ways can you move at the neck without rotating? [Four.] How many ways can you move at the ankle? [Four.] How many ways can you move at the knee? [One.] How many ways can you move at the hip? [Around in a circle; the hip is a ball joint similar to the shoulder.] How many ways can you move the back at the waist without rotating? [Four.] Now try the fingers and toes.

Go through the joints again using rotation. Rotation can best be felt at the shoulder and hip joints and along the spine at the neck and waist. Be sure the children discover the answers through movement.

11. As we sing the verse to "Dry Bones," move the bones we are singing about as conspicuously as possible. When we sing the chorus, rattle all your bones on different levels and in different directions, with changes in range, force, and speed just like a skeleton on Halloween.

This activity may also be done in groups with each group making up its own skeleton dance to the song. The song may be found in several song books listed in the Bibliography.

Muscles

12. Make a strong muscle-person shape. Tighten all your muscles so they bulge. Press your legs into the floor so your leg muscles contract. Now relax. Make a different muscle shape, relax your muscles, and freeze into a new muscle shape. Relax onto a new level and freeze in another muscle shape. Relax onto a different level again and try another muscle shape. Let us look at some of these muscle shapes.

13. Can you make just your right arm muscles work? Make a muscle in your right arm and have a friend check to see that all the other muscles in your body are loose. This is hard. Try doing it lying down. Try contracting different muscles in your body and keeping the rest of your muscles loose. Work with a friend who can check your muscles. Why is it important to be able to use just a few muscles instead of all your muscles all of the time? [If you have good muscle control, you will not waste your energy by using all your muscles for a task when just a few might be needed.] When might you just need to use your arm muscles or just your leg muscles or just one arm or one leg muscle?

14. Can you move through space using your muscles? Can you make strong, muscular jumps? Do they have to be loud? [No.] Try strong, muscular skips; gallops; runs; leaps; hops; walks; slides. Do your movements have to be big, slow, or loud to be strong? [No.] Try strong, muscular movements that are quick, soft, and small. Now try movements that do not use very

much muscle. Try looser, weaker skips, jumps, hops, runs, turns, and falls.

15. Find a partner. One of you be the skeleton and one the muscle. The skeleton should rattle its bones in many interesting ways, while the muscle moves in a strong way. Who is the skeleton and who is the muscle? We will guess when everyone has worked out their movements.

Body Parts

16. How many small body parts can you name and touch? How many large body parts can you name and touch?

    Variation: Flip a beanbag from hand to foot, head to back, knee to shoulder, wrist to ankle, etc.

17. Can you push your hand forward? your elbow backwards? your hips to the right? your shoulder to the left? your head up? your heels down? Who can tell the class the name of a body part and a direction in which to move it?

    Continue asking for ideas from the students. Try other movements such as bend, stretch, twist, swing, etc.

18. Pretend the room is dark except for a spotlight on your foot. Move that one body part in as many interesting ways as possible. You may move other parts of your body, but your foot should be the center of attention. Now try your shoulder. Do a shoulder dance. Can you do a knee dance? a finger dance? a back dance? a head dance?

    Continue with other body parts. Background music is helpful for this activity.

19. Can you use your arm as a sword? Slash it all about without touching anyone. Can your leg become a sword? you head? your back?

    Continue with other body parts becoming objects such as a pencil, whip, baseball bat, tennis racquet, noodle, etc.

20. Can you glue your back to the wall and move all your other body parts in many ways? Can you glue your knees to the floor and stretch your other body parts in different directions? Can you glue one hand to the floor and one foot to the wall and move the rest of your body with smooth, sustained movements? with jerky, percussive movements? with swinging movements? with vibrating movements? *(Continue with other body parts and different elements of movement.)*

21. Can you put your legs on a medium level and your head on a low level? Can you put your shoulders on a low level and your feet on a medium level? Can you put your head and legs on a low level and your stomach on a high level? *(Ask for similar challenges from the students.)*

22. Can you move *through* space on two hands and one foot? on your back? on your shoulders and feet? on two feet and one hand? on your stomach? on two knees and one hand? on one hand and one foot? on your buttocks? on one side of your body? Try moving in different directions.

Can you make a shape in which your hands and feet are on a low level and your back is on a medium level? These children devised a solution. ("The Body," Problem 21)

23. We are going to do a folk dance that uses body parts called "Looby Lou." *(Or use "The Hokey Pokey.")* When we come to the verse, each person will take a turn naming a body part to put into the circle. We will go around the circle. The person who is the leader will say, "I put my shoulder in." Then the rest of us will join in the verse using our shoulders. After the chorus, the next person in the circle will be the leader and will choose a body part for us to use. We will go around the circle until everyone has had a turn as the leader. Try to pick a body part that nobody else has used already.

Have the leader also decide on a locomotor movement for the chorus. The children will follow the leader's movements just as in "Follow the Leader."

The Five Senses

Sight

1. I am going to hold up a picture. Look at that picture and react to what you see through movement. What levels does the picture make you move on? In what directions do you feel like going? Does the picture give you any feelings of speed and force? Does the picture make you feel like moving in your self space or in general space? Answer these questions through movement.

   Hold up a variety of pictures that will evoke different responses. Ask the children to bring in pictures that affect them to use for this activity.

2. What does it feel like to be without sight? Close your eyes and make shapes on different levels. Can you balance on one body part with your eyes closed? on three body parts? on two body parts? on two different body parts?

   Let us form a circle. Now close your eyes and walk in toward the middle of the circle until you touch someone's shoulder. Walk backwards until you are at the spot where you think you started; then stop. Open your eyes and see where you are. What happened? Let us try that again. *(It helps to keep the shape of the circle if everyone takes tiny steps at the same tempo.)*

   Try many other movements with the eyes closed such as

turning, rocking, crawling, etc. Discuss the feelings and balance problems. Working with the eyes closed leads to greater kinesthetic awareness.

3. *(The children can do this activity seated at their desks or in a circle on the floor.)* Toss an eraser *(or beanbag)* from hand to hand. Focus on the eraser. That means look directly at the eraser as you toss it. Never take your eyes off the eraser. Now focus on your left hand, and only your left hand, as you toss the eraser. After several tosses, focus on your right hand. Now focus on the ceiling; on the floor; on the right wall; on the left wall; straight ahead; on a friend. Now close your eyes and try to toss and catch your eraser. When was it easiest to catch the eraser? [When focusing on the eraser.] When was it the most difficult? [Will vary with each child.] This experiment will help us remember to always focus on the object we are trying to catch.

4. *(You may use desks and erasers, balls and targets, beanbags and hoops, or wastebaskets for this activity.)* Let us do an experiment with throwing. Can you gently throw your eraser into your desk? Focus on your desk. Be sure you are looking at the desk and not at the eraser. Now focus on the eraser as you throw. Can you focus on the ceiling as you throw? on the floor? on the right wall? on the left wall? behind you? on a friend? straight ahead? Now try to get the eraser in the desk with your eyes closed. Where did you focus when you had the greatest success in getting the eraser in the desk? [When focusing on the desk.] When was it the hardest to hit the desk? [Answers will vary.] What can we deduce from this experiment? [When throwing at a target, always focus on the target.] Therefore, when catching, always focus on the object being caught. When throwing, always focus on the object you are aiming at.

5. Can you move across the room while focusing straight ahead? Move any way that you want to, but keep looking straight ahead. Now focus on the right wall but move straight ahead. Can you make a straight pathway? Try focusing on the left wall; on the floor; on the ceiling; on the corner; behind you. Try moving with your focus constantly changing. Look up, down, right, left, or up, right, down, left. Always try to keep a

straight pathway. Which was the easiest way to focus and keep a straight pathway? [Looking straight ahead.] Which was the hardest? [Answers will vary.] What have we learned from this experiment? [It is easiest and safest to look in the direction in which you are moving.]

6. Can you be someone's shadow? Find a partner and stand behind him or her. Your partner will be your leader. Follow your partner's movements exactly. You must focus on your partner at all times. Leader, try to think of many interesting shapes and movements as you move through general space. When I give the signal, change leaders.

7. We are going to do an experiment using focus in two ways. The performers will do focus problems "on stage" while the audience focuses on them. Then we will discuss the effect the performers' focus problem had on the audience. Let us begin. Can two people go to the front of the room and move while focusing on each other's eyes? Never look away from your partner's eyes as you move on different levels, etc. Now, audience, how did you feel while looking at that dance? Performers, how did you feel while doing the dance?

Can I have two more people up in front? Can these partners move and never look at each other? How did the audience feel while looking at that dance?

Continue in this fashion with the following problems: one focuses on the partner while the other focuses away; each focus on a body part of the other; both focus up; both focus down; one focuses up while the other focuses down; each focus on an opposite corner; both focus on someone in the audience; both focus out over the audience's heads; each focus on one of his or her own body parts. Each problem will have a different effect on the audience and the performers.

Hearing

8. *(Use a sound effects record for this problem or a similar tape you have made.)* I am going to play different sounds. Listen to what you hear and react to those sounds through movement. It doesn't matter if you know what the sound is or not. Just

listen and move the way the sound makes you feel like moving. *(Besides mechanical sounds, have the children listen and respond to animal and human sounds.)*

9. *(Use rhythm instruments for this activity.)* Each of you will play your instrument for a short time. The rest of us will listen to your instrument and move the way the instrument makes us feel. Try different tempos and volumes on your instrument.

10. Find a partner. *(This activity may also be done in groups or with the class as a whole.)* One of you make a repetitive nonsense sound with your voice or a body sound like clapping. The other person react to the sound through movement. Change roles after each sound.

11. What would you do if you heard a fire engine? Show me. What would you do if you heard whispering? screaming? laughing? shouting? cheering? crying? talking? singing? heavy breathing? sneezing?. coughing? whistling?

Listen to the instrument and move the way the sound makes you feel. ("The Five Senses," Problem 9)

It is fun to have one group make sounds for another group to react to. Switch roles after each sound.

12. How do you react to changes in someone's voice when they are talking directly to you? Find a partner. One of you be the talker and the other the listener-mover. The talker will say angry, kind, mean, sweet, rude, loving, scary, silly things to the partner. The partner will listen and react to these words through movement. Change roles after each speech. Notice how your partner reacts to what you say. Remember this is just an experiment.

13. *(See the problems in "Measurement:Music.")*

Taste

14. *(Bring in things to taste that are sweet, sour, bitter, salty, spicy, etc.)* Take a small taste of one of these foods. Show me your reactions through movement. Try another kind of food.

Show me through movement how the taste of the food makes you feel. These children are reacting to the taste of a lemon. ("The Five Senses," Problem 14)

Do you feel like moving differently? Why? How did your movements change? *(Continue with the rest of the food.)*

15. *(Divide the class into groups.)* Each group pick a food that you would like to describe through movement. Think about how you react when you eat the food. Exaggerate those actions and use the elements of movement to create a taste dance. We will try to guess each group's food when everyone is ready.

16. Think of tasting something you do not eat, such as sand. Can you show me how your whole body would react if you ate sand? mud? gravel? bark? worms? leaves? Are there any animals, insects, birds, or reptiles that eat the things we just explored? How does a bird react to tasting worms? Show me. Can you show me a beetle eating leaves? a worm eating mud; a beaver chewing bark? How did your reactions and movements change? What does this experiment show us?

Ask the children to name other foods that we do not eat, foods that other living things do eat, and vice versa. For example: how would a worm react to eating pizza?

17. Can you form two equal lines facing each other about eight feet apart? I am going to stand behind one line and hold up a food picture for the other line to see. The line facing the picture will make movements that show their reactions to tasting the food in the picture. The other line will try to guess what the food is by watching the movements. Then we will change roles. Remember to use your whole body when moving.

For example: You hold up a picture of a lemon. The students in the line facing the picture make movements that indicate they are tasting something tart. The opposing line guesses until someone says "lemon." Then you hold up a picture for the line that just guessed and the game continues.

Smell

18. *(Bring in different items like perfume, chili peppers, ammonia, pepper, and soap in unmarked bottles or bags.)* Open up one of the bottles carefully and smell the substance inside. Show your

reactions to what you smell with total body movement. *(Continue until all the items have been smelled and reacted to by the children.)*

19. What do you do when you smell smoke? Show me through movement. Use different levels, directions, range, force, and speed in your answers. Try to create a long movement phrase. What do you do when you smell fresh doughnuts? gasoline? rain? flowers? garbage? campfires? rotten eggs? peppermint?

20. What happens to your sense of smell when you have a cold and your nose is stuffed up? What happens to your sense of taste when your nose is stuffed up? How would you feel if you had a cold on Thanksgiving Day and couldn't smell or taste any of the food? Is your sense of smell important to you? Show me how you would feel if you lost it.

21. *(Divide the class into groups.)* Can you create a smell dance? Think of something to smell and show your reactions to that smell through movement. We will try to guess the smell each group is describing.

Touch

22. *(Bring little bags with an object in each one, or ask each child to bring a small interesting object to school.)* Exchange bags with a friend. Do not look inside. When it is your turn, put your hand in your bag and feel your object. Describe through movement the texture, size, weight, and shape of your object. The rest of us will try to guess what is in the bag. If you do not know what is in the bag, you may look. Then, when the class has guessed the correct object, we will go to the next person.

23. Find a partner. One of you close your eyes. The other will be the guide. The guide will lead his or her partner to a different place in the room. Can the person whose eyes are closed discover where he or she is by using the sense of touch? Do not open your eyes until you have correctly described your new place. Then change roles.

24. Find a partner and stand back-to-back just touching each

other. Can you slide across the room and stay together by using your sense of touch? Try sliding on different levels and with different speeds.

25. How would you feel if you touched something hot? Show me through movement. Touch something hot on a different level; on another level. Move in a different direction. How would you feel if you touched something cold? How did your range of movement change? your force? your tempo? Touch something sharp; something smooth. Touch something bumpy; something fluffy. Touch something hard; something soft. Touch something soggy; something crisp.

After each pair of objects, ask the children to compare the range, force, and speed of their movements. You might want to use actual objects as images to help motivate movement. For example: touch cooked spaghetti; touch potato chips. Encourage the children to use their whole bodies in their solutions.

26. *See Problem 4 in "Art: Materials and Textures" which uses different textured materials and the sense of touch.*

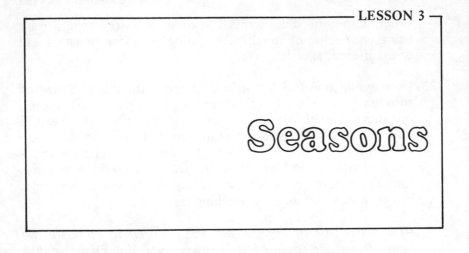

Seasons

Problems 1-6 deal with the seasons and the five senses.

1. Let's think about the seasons and the five senses. Can you show me through movement some of the smells of the fall season? of the winter season? of the spring season? of the summer season?

2. Think about your sense of taste. Show me how the taste of icicles and snow makes you feel. How do you feel while tasting a big Thanksgiving dinner? How does the taste of cold ice cream on a hot summer day make you feel? How does the first spring shower taste on your tongue?

3. What are some of the first signs of a new season that you can see? Think of a sign and a season. We will try to guess what each person is thinking of as we look at his or her movements.

4. What are some sounds that tell us fall is here? winter is here? spring is here? summer is here? Can you show me your reactions to these special sounds? Can you make the shape and movements of an object making one of the special sounds? Let's look at the different solutions and make a list of all the sounds that tell us a new season is here.

5. How can we use our sense of touch to tell us a new season is here? Show me how the pavement feels on your bare feet in the summer; in the winter. How does the texture of the grass

change with the seasons? Can you show me through movement? How does the sun feel on your skin in summer? the rain
in spring? the snow in winter? the wind in fall? How does the
texture of your clothes change over the seasons? Can you
show me through movement?

6. *(Divide the class into groups of five or more.)* Each group pick
a season to describe through movement. Describe your season
using the five senses. Show us how your season tastes, smells,
sounds, looks, and feels. When every group is ready, we will
look at each group and try to guess the season they are
describing.

7. What do some animals do in the fall? [Store food for winter,
get fat, grow more fur, migrate to warmer climates.] Can you
show me through movement?

What do some animals do in the winter? How many animals
that hibernate can you describe through movement? Can you
show me?

What do most adult animals do in the spring? [Give birth to
babies.] Can you show me how a baby chick might look
hatching out of its shell? What are other animals that hatch
from eggs in the spring? Show me. Let's look at some of the
solutions and try to guess what animals are hatching.

What do animals do in the summer? [Eat, play, raise their
young.] Choose an animal and show me some of its summer
activities.

8. How do plants change with the seasons? What do plants do in
the spring? Think of a particular flower or vegetable or tree.
Show me what happens to your plant in the spring. Let's look
and guess the names of the plants we see growing.

How do plants look in the summer? What can happen to plants
that get too much sun and not enough water? Show me. How
do plants change when fall comes? Show me.

How do many plants look in the winter? Do any plants bloom
and grow in the winter season? Where? [In warm climates.]

Can you think of any plants in these areas and describe them through movement?

9. How do your activities change with each season? What are some activities you do mainly in the fall? Show me. What activities do you do mainly in the winter? in the spring? in the summer? Can you do any of these activities during other seasons—besides the one you thought of—without going to a different area of the world? Show me. Show me what activities can be done in any season.

Can you show me an activity that you do in the winter? With the help of some classmates, this student is building a snowman. ("The Seasons," Problem 9)

10. Do we live in a place that has four different seasons? Does everyone live in a place with as many seasons as we have? Do some people have more or fewer seasons? Show me how you would feel if you lived in a place that had only two seasons: winter and fall; spring and summer; winter and summer; spring and fall.

If the children live in an area with less than four seasons, ask them how they would react to four different seasons.

Weather

1. How is a cloud formed? Can you show me step by step through movement? First drops of water must rise into the air. Where does the water come from? [From many places.] Pick one place and show me. Are you an ocean, river, lake, pond, puddle, stream, dew, glass of water? Let's look at all the different places where water appears. Now the sun comes out and shines on your water. What happens? Show me. As your water vapor rises, the air gets cooler and cooler. What will happen? Can you show me your drops getting cooler and forming a big cloud?

   If you have discussed various cloud formations, ask the class to make the shapes of the different formations. This activity may also be done in groups with each group forming one cloud of many individual water drops.

2. How does it feel to move through fog? Let us pretend the room is full of thick fog. Move across the room as you show me the answers to my questions. Is the fog warm or cool? How wet is it? How well can you see?

   Do you know what fog is? [A cloud low to the ground.] I will divide the class in half. One half will be the water drops that form the fog. The other half will be travelers trying to get home in the fog. The fog will move slowly around the room making it difficult for the travelers to get home. Travelers, decide what kind of transportation you are going to use. Then use that transportation, trying to avoid the fog until you reach your desk (or wall) safely. When everyone is home safely we will change roles.

Variation: Make the fog thicker and thicker by decreasing the size of area the children move in. Ask the water drops to move only in their self space, glued to one spot, and see if they can reach out to touch a traveler. Each game they will move to a new spot closer together. The travelers will have to decrease their range of movement and their speed. Bring out in a discussion the idea that the heavier the fog is, the slower you should go.

3. What happens when a cloud becomes cool? [Rain falls.] Start out in an interesting cloud shape floating high in the air. The temperature drops. What will happen? Show me. Make a new cloud shape. This time try to find a partner water drop on the way down and form a large raindrop together. Can you get together with three people now? four people? Can the whole class come together to form a giant raindrop and fall to the ground? *(This is a good exercise in spatial awareness and group cooperation.)*

4. What will happen if the temperature drops way down and your cloud becomes very, very cold? [Snowflakes form.] Show me through movement. How does the snow fall compared to the rain? [More slowly and more lightly.] Show me. How is the shape of a snowflake different from a raindrop? Show me. Can you show me many different snowflake shapes? Each time your shape hits the ground and melts, rise up in a new snowflake shape, float, and fall again. Keep floating, falling, and rising in new shapes. Let us watch half of the class at a time to see all the interesting snowflakes. *(This is a good exercise for learning to sink and rise gracefully and easily, which is helpful in preventing injuries when falling.)*

5. What is hail? [Frozen raindrops.] Show me hail falling from the sky. Every time you hit the ground, rise and form a new hailstone.

Let us compare the force, shape, and speed of rain, snow, and hail. First, be rain falling from the sky. Think of how rain feels as it hits your face. Is it hard, soft, warm, cold? Does it fall quickly or slowly? There are different kinds of rainstorms. First be rain falling in a summer shower. Now be rain in a heavy thunderstorm. The force and speed of the drops should change.

Now try snow. What is the shape, speed, and force of your snowflakes?

Now try hail. How is the hail different from rain and snow? [Hail is heavier, harder, and falls with more speed than rain or snow.]

6. *(Divide the class into groups.)* I am going to give each group a type of weather to portray. Some of you might want to be the weather while others show their reactions to you. You might all be the weather, or you might all be people caught in the weather. We will try to guess what type of weather each group is portraying and how they are portraying it.

Give conditions such as: drought, hot humid day, thunderstorm, summer shower, heavy fog, blizzard, light snow, cold crisp day, etc.

7. Weather affects us in several ways. One thing it affects is your mood. How do you feel on a hot, muggy day? Show me through movement. Try to use different directions and pathways as you move. How do you feel on a cold, snowy day? Try to use different levels and speed as you move.

How do you feel on a cool, rainy day? on a foggy day? on a warm, dry day? in a tornado? Try to make interesting shapes as you move. Use different locomotor and nonlocomotor movements. Let us look at some people moving and try to guess what type of weather they are thinking about.

Let the children suggest other weather conditions that affect their moods. This activity may be done in groups with each group choosing a type of weather and showing how it affects their moods. The other groups enjoy guessing the weather and its effect.

8. Weather reports and forecasts are very important. Who are

How do you feel on a cold, rainy day? The moods of these children are obvious! ("Weather," Problem 7)

some of the people for whom these forecasts are important? [Pilots, farmers, ranchers, food packers, power companies, sailors, resort owners, explorers, astronauts, etc.] Think of one group of people that rely on weather forecasts and describe the group through movement. We will look at the solutions and make a list of all the people who rely on weather forecasts.

9. Some people do rain dances when they need rain. Can you make up a dance to bring on some particular kind of weather? Could you do a sun dance or snow dance or fog dance? Choose the weather you would like to have and create a dance to produce your weather. We will try to guess what each person is dancing about. Try to make your movement and shapes depict the weather you desire. *(The older children enjoy creating a dance together in groups.)*

10. *(Divide the class into groups for this activity.)* Many proverbs about weather have been handed down over the years. I am going to give each group a card with a proverb written on it. Think of a way to describe your proverb through movement. Try to use all the elements of movement—space, time, force, and flow. When each group is ready, we will watch their movement phrase and try to think of the proverb they are describing. We will also discuss whether a proverb is true or false.

The proverbs and their validity can be discussed before this activity so that the children are familiar with them. The following proverbs are examples of some that might be used:
   a. When ants travel in a straight line, expect rain; when they scatter, expect fair weather. [False.]
   b. A tough apple skin means a hard winter. [Possible.]
   c. When bees stay close to the hive, rain is close by. [True.]
   d. Geese fly higher in fair weather than in foul. [True.]
   e. Sea gull, sea gull sit on the sand; it's sign of a rain when you are at hand. [True.]

For more proverbs and their explanations see Folklore of American Weather *by Eric Sloane.*

11. *(Before doing this activity read the Dr. Seuss book* Bartholomew and the Oobleck *to the children.)* In the story I just read there was a new kind of precipitation. An awful green sticky substance fell from the sky. Can you invent a new kind of weather condition? Give it a name and show through movement its shape, weight, texture, speed, and how it affects people. When everyone is ready, we will look at all the new kinds of weather.

The class might want to react through movement to some of the weather that was created. This activity may also be done in groups with one group providing the magical weather for another group of startled townspeople.

Plants

1. We have been growing plants from seeds. Can you imitate the growth of our corn plant? How did the seed first look before we put it in wet cotton? Show me through movement. What was the first thing that happened? [A root appeared.] Show me. What happened next? [A little plant appeared.] In which direction did the roots go? In which direction did the plant go? Show me. What happened after several more days? [The leaves grew and opened up.] Can you show me? How does the cornstalk look when the corn is ready to be picked and eaten? Show me. Where are the seeds to plant for next year's crop? *(Repeat the activity for other seeds of different shapes such as bean, pea, etc.)*

2. What do plants need to grow? Yes, air is one thing. How can you show me air through movement? Where does air travel? on what levels? [All levels.] in what directions? with what speed? with what force? Show me many kinds of air: air on a very windy day; air on a hot, still summer day; air on a cool, breezy day.

   What else do plants need? [Water.] What ways do plants get water? Can you show me many ways? [From a sprinkler, hose, water can, river, lake, pond, ocean, rain, etc.]

   What else do plants need for growth? [Soil.] Can you show me different kinds of soil? How would frozen soil look? muddy soil? dry, cracked soil? rocky soil? sandy soil? good topsoil?

Can you describe through movement a plant beginning to sprout from its seed? ("Plants," Problem 1)

Plants also need sunlight. Can you show me how the sun shines on plants?

3. Can you grow plants only from seeds? What else produces plants? [Bulbs, roots, underground stems, and cuttings.] Let us go through the list. Can you make each type of plant and then show me something the plant produces? We will try to guess the plants to see if they are in the right family.

For example, a child might make the shape of a bulb and then a tulip. If the child makes a bulb and then a sweet potato, a brief review of bulb plants would be in order.

4. Are all the seeds in the world planted or scattered by man? How else are seeds scattered? Who can name four ways? [By wind, water, animals, and gravity.]

   Let me see you be the wind carrying a seed to a new location. What levels, directions, pathways, speed, and force can you use?

   Show the water carrying a seed to a new home. What travels by water that could scatter seeds? [Boats.] Show me.

   Choose an animal that might carry a seed to a new location and show me your choice through movement. What is another way an animal could carry a seed to a new place? Show me.

   Can you be a seed pulled to the ground by gravity? What kind of seed are you? What will you grow into? Show me. Let us look at some of these solutions and discuss them.

5. I am going to put a list of plants we eat on the board. *(You may want to use pictures for the younger children.)* Do you know which are roots, stems, bulbs, or mainly leaves? If the plant is mainly leaves, make an *L* with your body. Make an *R* for roots; an *S* for stems and a *B* for bulbs.

   Variations: (a) Make the shape of a leaf, stem, root, or bulb. (b) Assign an action to each type such as leap for leaf, bend for bulb, stretch for stem, and rock for roots.

6. *(This activity can be done in groups with older children or in a single unit with younger children.)* What important things are made from plants? I will write some headings on the board as you name them. *(Write down such headings as food, medicine, building materials, cloth etc.)*

   Can you describe through movement an item that would fit under each heading on the board? Try to move in and through space instead of just freezing in a shape. We will look at the solutions and write the items shown under the correct headings on the board. *(If the children are working in groups, have them make as many items for each heading as possible.)*

Animals

1. What are some animals that move low to the ground? Can you show me? I see snakes, crocodiles, alligators, turtles, ants. Let's divide the room in half so that everyone can see each other's animals. Now try making the shape and movements of another animal that moves low to the ground.

   Can you make the shape and movements of an animal that is tall or moves in the sky? I see birds, giraffes, elephants, dinosaurs, butterflies. Let's watch each other again.

   Now try making the shape of an animal that moves neither low to the ground nor high in the sky. I see horses, dogs, cats, deer, hippopotamuses.

   Can some animals move on more than one level? [Birds move on the ground, giraffes can lie down, insects can crawl up trees, etc.] Choose an animal and show all the different levels it can move on.

2. *(A discussion of animals along with a display of pictures is helpful in motivating movement.)* Can you think of some animals that can move very quickly? Show me their shapes, size, and speed through movement. Let's watch one-half of the class at a time and discuss the animals we see.

   What are some animals that move slowly? Show me through movement. Does size make a difference as to whether an animal can move slowly or not? [No, elephants can move quickly, turtles cannot, fish can move quickly, hippopotamuses cannot.] What does make a difference in determining an animal's speed? [Type of animal, type of body build, and whether it uses its speed for survival or whether it has other means of protection, such as the porcupine.]

Ask the children to try several differently shaped fast- and slow-moving animals.

3. What are some animals that are very strong? Can you be an elephant moving a giant tree trunk? Can you be a boa constrictor squeezing a tree trunk? Can you show me other strong animals? When are animals weak? [When they are born, undernourished, sick, wounded, tired, etc.] Can you show me the shape and movements of a weak animal? Try to describe through your movements the cause for your animal's weakness.

4. Let's think about the quality of movement certain animals have. How does a member of the cat family move when it is stalking its prey? [Slow, sustained, sinuous movements.] How does it move when it pounces? [Quick, percussive movements.] Show me.

How does a rattlesnake move slithering through the grass? Show me. How does the rattler's movements change as it gets ready to strike? What kind of movements does the snake use to strike out at its prey? Show me. [Sustained, vibratory, and percussive force.] Can you show me how an elephant moves as it walks through the forest? [Head, trunk, and tail swing back and forth.]

How does a monkey move from tree to tree? How does a hummingbird move its wings?

Continue working on this problem using other animals. Encourage the children to use the four qualities of force— sustained, percussive, vibratory, and swing—to help describe the animals' movement characteristics.

5. Let's create a zoo. Who would like to make the shape, movements, and characteristics of animals in the reptile house?

in the small mammal house? in the aviary? in the amphibian house? in the aquarium? in the large mammal house? in the insect house? When everyone is ready, we will watch each house, guess the animals we see, and decide if they are all in the right place. *(This activity reinforces the concept of what animals belong to which class.)*

6. What animals can be trained to perform? [Elephants, horses, lions, tigers, dogs, monkeys, porpoises, parrots, seals, bears.] Let's create a circus. Think of an animal that can perform tricks and show the class your animal and its tricks. The class will try to guess your animal. When everyone has shown an animal, let's put similar animals together to perform in a ring. After each different group of animals has performed, we will discuss what we saw.

7. Let's make a list of animals that are classified as endangered species. Choose an animal on that list to research. Find out the animal's eating habits, ways of protecting itself, sleeping habits, why it is an endangered species, etc. When you have your information, portray your animal through movement for the class and be prepared to discuss your research.

8. Can you show me animals that live in the desert? in winter climates? in rain forests? in jungles? on mountains? in ponds? in oceans? underground? in trees? on farms?

9. What are some ways in which animals protect themselves from their enemies? Can you show me what a cat uses? [Claws.] Move around the room as a cat might move fighting off an enemy. What are some other animals that use claws? Think of one and show me its shape, size, and movements as it fights off the enemy.

What does a bull, elk, or rhinoceros use for protection? [Horns.] Can you show me? Can you think of other animals that use horns?

What do some insects, birds, and small mammals use for protection? [Flight.] Can you show me a fly trying to get away from the fly swatter? a robin trying to get away from a cat? a squirrel trying to get away from a dog?

Can you show me ways in which animals protect themselves? The boys
in the foreground are horned bulls; the girl in the center is a poisonous
snake; and the children in the background are birds in flight. ("Animals," Problem 9)

What are some animals that protect themselves with poison?
[Bees, snakes, jellyfish, some spiders.] Can you show me
where the poison comes from on each animal?

What animals use odor? [Skunks.] Show me one of these
animals fighting off an enemy.

What animals use their body surfaces as protection? [Porcu-
pines, shellfish, turtles, tortoises, armadillos, stingrays, etc.]
Think of one and make the shape, size, movements, and
protective covering of your animal. We will look at each
other's solutions and discuss what we see.

How do dogs, wolves, crocodiles, sharks, and similar animals
protect themselves? [With their teeth.] Show me through
movement.

Do you know how a chameleon protects itself? [By changing color.] What other animals use color as a means of protection? [Polar bear, ermine, butterfly, many small mammals, insects, and fish.] Can you choose one of those animals to portray through movement?

What are some animals that use unusual ways to protect themselves? [Electric eel, boa constrictor, octopus, spiders, vampire bats, squids.]

10. How are baby chicks born? [Hatched from eggs.] Can you be a little baby chicken breaking out of its egg and moving for the first time? *(It is helpful to show a film or let the children see real chicks hatching before doing this activity.)*

What other animals are hatched from eggs? [Fish, insects, birds, reptiles, amphibians.] How many different baby animals that are hatched from eggs can you show me? Let's make a list of all the animals you are portraying.

11. Do you know the name for a group of fish? [A school.] Who can get together with some friends to move as a school of fish might move? Let's make a list of the names for other groups of animals.

Some examples of animal groups are: litter of pups, flock of sheep, swarm of bees, brood of hens, string of ponies, covey of partridges, plague of locusts, colony of ants, murder of crows, pod of seals, rafter of turkeys, gam of whales, pride of lions, nest of robins, gang of elk, crash of rhinoceroses, drove of cattle, gaggle of geese, troop of kangaroos, and parliament of owls.

Can you get together with a group of friends and choose one or two groups of animals to portray for the class? Try to portray the meaning of the name of the group besides just making the shape of the animal.

For more examples of animal group names, see An Exhaltation of Larks *by James Lipton.*

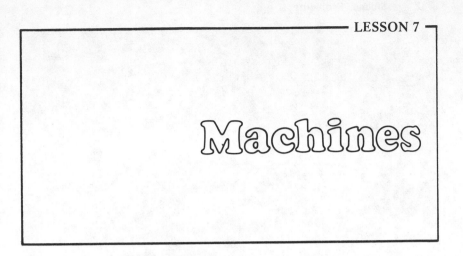

Machines

The first set of problems is based on the six simple machines: lever, wheel, pulley, inclined plane, screw, and wedge.

1. Show the class pictures of different levers, such as crowbar, scissors, sugar or ice tongs, wheelbarrow, teeter-totter, etc.

   Can you become one of the levers you see in the pictures? Can you be a crowbar pulling a big nail out of the floor? Can your leg be the crowbar? your arm? your finger? your whole body?

2. Let us try scissors. Can your arms be scissors cutting a big piece of paper? your legs? an arm and a leg? Can you cut paper on a low level with your arms? on a high level with your legs? Can you find a partner and make a giant pair of scissors?

3. Find a partner and make a wheelbarrow. Can you push your wheelbarrow in a curved pathway? a zigzag pathway? a straight pathway? Can you pull the wheelbarrow backwards? push it forwards?

4. Show me how a teeter-totter looks. How would a teeter-totter move if two people the same size sat on each end? What would happen if a big person sat on one end and a little person on the other? Show me. How could we get the teeter-totter to move? [Move the big person closer to the middle.]

5. Let us try the sugar and ice tongs. Turn your body into ice

181

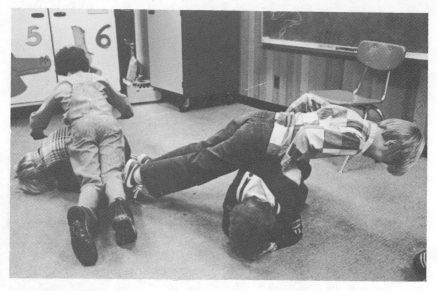

Can you show me how a teeter-totter moves? ("Machines," Problem 4)

tongs. Show me how you would pick up a giant block of ice. What kind of force are you using? [Strong.] Now be a sugar tongs and pick up a little sugar cube. What kind of force are you using? [Weak.]

Make up other problems similar to problems 1-5 for the other five kinds of simple machines, using the elements of space, time, force, and flow.

6. Think of all the tools you would need to build a treehouse. I will write the tools on the chalkboard as you name them. Let us say that these are magical tools because they do not need anybody to make them work; they work by themselves. Can you show me how these magical tools would build a treehouse? I might see saws sawing and hammers hammering among many other things.

7. *(Have one of your students or a group of students make a tape of machine sounds or use a record for this problem.)* I am going to play a tape of machine sounds. Listen to the sounds and become the machine that you think you hear on the tape. Remember to move on different levels, in different directions,

etc. Let us divide the class in half and look at the machines you are making.

8. Now make up your own sounds for your machine. Can we guess what your machine is from your actions and sounds?

9. I am going to divide the class into groups and give each group the name of a place in the city. Think of machines found in this place. Work individually to create different machines. When you are done, we will guess what machines you are making.

Give categories such as: office, fire station, train station, building a skyscraper, harbor, a plant, etc. You may also give more general categories such as machines found on a farm, in the city, in the house, in the air, on the water, on the land.

10. Each group will create one big machine. Can each individual within the group be a simple machine that is part of the big

Can your group think of an office machine and describe it through movement? This group is making a computer. ("Machines," Problem 9)

machine? We should be able to see levers, wheels, screws, wedges, pulleys, etc., all working together to create one big machine. *(You may want to give categories from which groups can choose a machine.)*

11. Can you make up a magical machine? A machine no one has invented before? Think of a name for it, and we will try to guess what your machine does when you are through. *(Direct students to work individually or in groups.)*

12. Let us think of how machines have changed through the ages. How did people first wash clothes? [Rubbing them against rocks in a stream, perhaps.] Can you show me those actions?

What was introduced next? [A washboard, which is an inclined plane.] Can you show me that object and how it was used?

What did the first washing machine look like? What simple machines made up the big washing machine?

What does a modern washing machine look like and how does it work? Find some friends and show me a working modern washer. Can you show me what simple machines are found in this big machine?

Try other machines to show how they have become more complex: airplanes, farm equipment, boats, cars, tools, lawn mowers, fishing equipment, building machines, etc. Picture books can be very helpful for ideas.

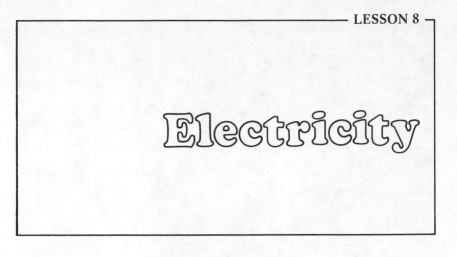

Electricity

1. What are three ways that electricity works for us? I will write each way you name on the board. [Heat, light, and motion.] What appliances that produce heat in your home are run by electricity? Think of one appliance and describe it through movement. We will look at the appliances when everyone is ready and write the objects you have made under the word *heat* on the board. *(Some possible appliances are: irons, ranges, toasters, heaters, dryers.)*

   Continue in the same fashion for light *and* motion.

2. Where does electricity come from? Generators in power plants produce electric current. But what makes generators run? Water can be used to run a generator. Can you show me how? Coal can be used to run a generator. What happens to the coal so that it can run a generator? Show me [Coal burns, producing steam that drives a turbine which drives a generator.]

   Can you think of other things besides generators that can produce electricity? Show me. [Dry-cell battery, wet-cell battery, solar battery, and atomic reactors.]

3. What objects can conduct electricity? I have written a list of objects on the board. *(Use objects such as string, pencil, nail, coin, straw, paper clip, rubber band, etc.)* Make the shape of one of the objects that you think can conduct electricity. Then we will test the real object with our dry-cell battery and

What things that produce light are run by electricity? This group is describing a car's headlights and taillights. ("Electricity," Problem 1)

light bulb to see if it can actually conduct electricity. *(See Diagram 11.)*

4. Why is copper wire used to conduct electricity? [Because the copper atom loses electrons easily.] Can the whole class form a copper atom to demonstrate the availability of the copper atom electrons? First we need a nucleus. Now we need two electrons for the inside orbit, eight for the next larger orbit, and eighteen for the third orbit. The outside orbit has one electron that wanders off and is replaced by a second electron that also wanders off. When the wire carries electricity, the electrons will not move at random. Instead, many electrons will rush in the same direction—from one end of the wire to another. Let us demonstrate this principle through movement.

5. Why doesn't rubber conduct electricity? [Because the atoms in rubber hold on to their electrons.] What do we use rubber for? [To insulate copper wire.] What would happen if you touched a live electric wire that was not insulated? Show me through

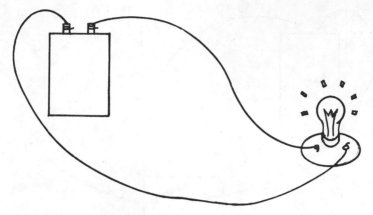

Diagram 11. ("Electricity," Problems 3 and 6)

movement. *(A discussion on safety in connection with electricity might follow this activity.)*

6. *(Divide the class into small groups.)* Can you show me how a dry cell can be used to produce electricity? Think of a simple object that needs electricity to work, such as a light bulb. Someone be that object and the rest of you produce electric current to make the object work. What will you need? *(See Diagram 11: dry cell with two screws, two wires, and bulb mounted in a fixture with two screws.)* Make the shapes of the objects you need and show how the bulb is made to light up. We will look at the groups to see if everything is connected correctly.

7. *(Divide the class into groups.)* Can each group demonstrate how an electric switch works? *(See Diagram 12.)* What objects will the individuals in each group have to make? [A dry cell, three wires, light bulb, switch holder, switch, and a metal strip.] Have someone in each group turn the switch on and off so the process will be demonstrated. We will watch each group when everyone is ready.

8. *(Divide the class into groups.)* Can each group make an electromagnet? Does it matter how many turns of wire are used? [Yes, the more turns the stronger the magnet.] Decide what sort of objects you want to pick up; then determine how

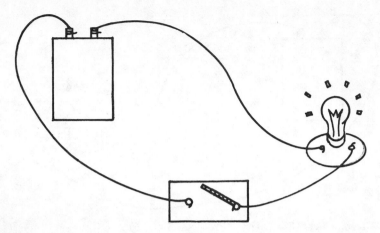

Diagram 12. ("Electricity," Problem 7)

many turns of wire you might need. Show what happens when you turn off the current. Does the nail stop being a magnet immediately or does it take time? When everyone is ready, we will watch each group to see how they answered my questions.

9. *(Divide the class into groups.)* Can each group demonstrate how the school bell works? What do you need to make the bell ring that you did not need to make the bulb light up? [Electromagnets.] If you have enough people in your group, make several dry cells and a switch so the bell will ring loudly and turn on and off. We will look at each group to see how they solved this problem when everyone is ready.

10. *(Divide the class into groups.)* I am going to give each group a card with a place written on it. *(Factory, home, store, office, hospital, broadcasting studio, etc.)* Think of an object or objects that are run by electricity and can be found in your place. Your group can work together to make one or two large objects, or individuals and pairs may form many different objects. When everyone is ready, we will try to guess the electrical objects and the place in which the objects are found.

Variation: When working with young children, give the whole class one category and ask for individual responses. Divide the class in half to view and discuss the different solutions; then proceed to the next category.

Magnets

1. I am going to turn you all into magnets that have only south poles. Move around the room and show me what happens when you get near another person. Move on different levels, in different directions, and with changes in speed. What will happen if I turn you all into magnets that have only north poles? [The magnets will again repel each other.]

2. Decide whether you want to be the north pole of a magnet or the south pole of a magnet. If you are the north pole, point your fingers upward. If you are the south pole, point your fingers downward. Move about the room in different, interesting ways and show me what happens as you get near other magnets. [When the north pole magnets meet the south pole magnets, they stick together.]

3. What are magnets used for? Think of one use and describe it through movement. [Compasses, picking up scrap iron, electric bells, picking up small metal objects, tape for sound, naval mines, etc.]

4. *See problems 8 and 9 in "Electricity."*

5. Make the shape of an object that can be picked up by a magnet. Pretend you are being moved about the room by a giant electromagnet. Listen to my drum beats *(or clapping)*. As the beats get slower, the electricity get less powerful. Your objects begin to lose their magnetism and become weaker and weaker until they are lying on the ground.

Planets, Moon, Stars

Earth

1. How does the earth move? Can you show me with your body? What shape is the earth? Can you make a round shape and turn as the earth turns? Does the earth stay in one place and turn, or does it move through space while it is turning? Can you turn your body around in a circle and move through space? Try to turn and move across the room.

   Do you know what kind of pathway the earth moves in? That is right. The earth moves in a curved pathway. Now, can you keep turning your body and move through space in a big curved pathway?

   This is challenging for young children. You might draw a big chalk circle on the floor for the children to follow.

2. When do you know it is daytime on the earth? When do you know it is nighttime? Does the sun stop shining at nighttime? No, the sun always shines, but one-half of the earth turns away from the sun.

   Who would like to be the sun? Can you make a large shape and make movements that show us you are always shining, always making light?

   Now we need an earth. How does the earth move in relationship to the sun? Does the earth move through the sun, over the sun, under the sun? Good, it moves around the sun. Can the earth turn very slowly around the sun and also around in its own circle?

Let us pretend we live on this human earth's nose. When the earth's nose is facing the sun, are we in daylight or darkness? Now, the earth's nose is away from the sun. Are we in daylight or darkness?

Find a partner. One of you be the sun and one of you be the earth. The earth will pick a place on his or her body that is "home." As the earth moves around the sun, discuss between you whether "home" is in daylight or darkness. Then change roles.

Variation: Have the older children try to determine approximately what time it is at "home," using the earth's relationship to the sun as a guide.

3. *(You need a strong light or projector for this activity.)* I need about six people to join together to form the earth. The bright light from this projector will be the sun. Can the earth stay in its self space and turn around in a circle? Who is in sunlight? Who is in darkness? Can you tell what time of day it is for each child as he or she stays still? Now the earth should turn again. Who is coming into daylight? Who is going into darkness? *(Continue with similar questions and other groups of children.)*

4. *(Divide the class into groups.)* Can you form the earth with your group? Try to show as many different features of the earth as possible. Can you make clouds, trees, oceans, mountains on your earth? When everyone is ready, we will look at the earths and discuss what we see.

Moon

5. How many moons does the earth have? Can you make the shape of a full moon? How does the moon move and where does it move? It is easier to be the moon than the earth because the moon only moves around itself once for each circle around the earth.

Find a partner. One of you be the moon and one be the earth. Stay in one spot, but as the earth moves around itself, the moon should move around the earth. Moon, remember to only move one full body turn as you go around the earth.

Now, let us add the sun. Find a third person to work with. Can the earth move around the sun while the moon is moving around the earth? Let's try it. When you have done this once, change roles.

6. How does the moon change shape? Can you show me a crescent moon? a half-moon? a three-quarter or gibbous moon? a full moon? Try those different shapes on different levels.

7. How many phases does the moon have altogether? [Eight.] Find a partner. One be the earth and one be the moon. Can the moon change phases as it moves once around the earth? The moon should make eight shapes before it gets back to its starting point. Think of a shape for the new moon that is different from the full moon. Change roles after the moon has made one trip.

8. What temperatures are on the moon? Can you make a moon shape and do movements that describe the temperatures found on the moon? Can you make boiling movements on one half of your body and freezing movements on the other half?

9. What is the surface of the moon like? [Dry, rocky, and dusty, with mountains and craters.] Can you describe the surface of the moon through movement?

10. How do the astronauts move on the moon? What would you feel like without gravity pulling you down? Show me through movement. Can you try all the locomotor movements you know and pretend you are doing them on the moon?

11. *(Divide the class into groups.)* Create a moon with your group. Show me the shape, surface, temperatures, and orbit of the moon through movement.

12. *(Divide the children into pairs. You need one ball for each pair*

Can you land a rocket on the moon? The child with the ball represents the earth trying to project a rocket to the moon, which is represented by the other child. ("Planets, Moon, Stars," Problem 12)

of children.) The person with the ball will be the earth. The other person will be the moon. The earth is going to try to send a rocket to the moon. The ball will be the rocket. The moon will move quickly in its orbit around the earth. Earth, as the moon passes in front of you, roll your rocket at it. Did your rocket land on the moon? [Probably not.] Why not? [By the time the ball reached the moon, the moon had moved to a new place.]

What do you have to do to land the rocket on the moon? Are you going to aim in front of or behind the moon? [In front.] Try to land your rocket again. After three tries, change roles.

Include these points in a discussion following the problem: scientists must know how fast the rocket is going, how fast the moon is going, and the distance between the moon and the earth before they can land a rocket on the moon.

The Other Planets

13. Can you show me through movement what the planet Mercury is like? What are its temperatures? its surface? its size? its shape?

14. How is Venus different from Mercury? Can you show me the traces of oxygen and water on your planet? How is the temperature different? the size?

15. What is distinctive about Mars? [Polar caps.] Can you show me?

16. Can you describe Jupiter through movement? How big is it? What kind of surface do you think it has? What are its temperatures?

17. What does Saturn have that no other planet in our system has? [Rings.] Can you show me as you move your planet in its orbit through space?

18. How are Uranus, Neptune, and Pluto similar? [All are far from the sun and very cold.] Choose one of those three planets and describe it through movement.

19. *(Divide the class in half.)* Can each half describe our solar system through movement? Try to make each of the nine planets distinctive, since they each have their own characteristics. Can you show the different sizes and their distances from the sun and each other? Extra people can be moons, Saturn's rings, or meteors. Do not forget the sun. Do not forget to rotate or to move in your orbits. When everyone is ready, we will look at the two solar systems and discuss what we see.

20. *(Divide the class into groups.)* Can each group create its own solar system? There are many other solar systems in the universe besides ours. Create new planets to describe through movement. Think of your size, surface, shape, temperature, rotational speed, and orbital path. What is special about your planet? Show us through movement. Give your planet a name. When each group has worked out its solar system, we will take a space voyage into the unknown to visit the new planets.

Stars

21. *(Divide the class into groups.)* Choose a constellation that we have been studying and form the constellation with your group. The rest of us will try to guess your constellation.

    Variations: (a) Give each group a card with a constellation pictured on it for the group to copy through movement and name. (b) With young children, form constellations under your guidance, one at a time, in front of the class.

Eclipse

22. Let's demonstrate a lunar eclipse through movement. We need a sun, moon, and earth. Who can tell these three people how and where to move so that a lunar eclipse will occur?

    After the eclipse has been demonstrated, divide the class into

Can your group describe a lunar eclipse through movement? ("Planets, Moon, Stars," Problem 22)

groups of three. Can each group make its own lunar eclipse occur? Try making your lunar eclipse on different levels.

23. What three people can demonstrate a solar eclipse for the class? Now everyone find two people to work with and create a solar eclipse with your trio. What is the difference between a lunar and solar eclipse? [A solar eclipse occurs when the moon passes between the earth and sun and blocks our view of the sun. A lunar eclipse occurs when the earth's shadow is cast upon the moon as the earth passes between the sun and moon.]

Gravity

1. Can you jump up in the air? What happened? The earth's gravity pulled you down. Jump as high as you can. What did you do to work against gravity and jump up high? [Bent the knees deeply and used the arms.] What do you have to do with your legs when gravity pulls you down from your high jump? [Bend the knees deeply to absorb the force created.] How else can you move against gravity's pull? Show me. [Hopping, leaping, and moving in many ways on an inclined plane.]

2. Throw something up in the air (an eraser, ball, beanbag, or crumpled piece of paper). What happened? Did it fly away? No, gravity pulled it back down. Toss your object again. How many times can you clap before gravity pulls it back down? How many times can you turn around? jump up and down? punch? swing your arm?

    How can you throw a ball high into the air? Try some different ways and think of what your body is doing to work against gravity. *(If you use as many body parts as possible and a wide range of movement, more force will be created.)*

    Now think about the speed of the ball. Does the ball come down faster if it is thrown high or low, or does it fall at the same speed every time you throw it? Try an experiment. Throw the ball a very short distance into the air. Keep your hands open, palms up, and let the ball fall down and slap your hands. Think about how that felt. Now throw the ball as high

197

as you can. Hold your hands out and let the ball slap them. Which time did the ball hit the hardest? [After it was thrown up high.] Can you tell from this experiment whether falling things keep the same speed or do they get faster or slower? [Faster.]

3. *(This is a good activity to use when children are tense or excited.)* Can you stretch way up to the sky? Now relax and let gravity pull all your body parts to the ground. Stretch up and let gravity pull just your right arm down; your left arm; your head; shoulders; back; knees; whole body.

   Lie down on the floor on your back and let your muscles relax. Let gravity take over. Let your arms feel heavy and sink into the floor. Let your legs sink into the floor; your back; your neck and head. Let your jaw drop open. Feel gravity pulling you down. Relax until I give you the signal to sit up.

4. Balance on five body parts; then let gravity take over, fall, roll, and stand up. Balance on four body parts, fall, roll, and stand up. Try that with three body parts; two body parts; one body part.

   Now try moving through space. Run, tip, collapse, roll. Run, tip, collapse, roll. When you feel gravity pulling you down, relax and roll on the side of your thigh and shoulder. Do not land on your knees.

   Try different combinations such as: jump, run, collapse, roll; gallop, turn, collapse, roll; skip, stretch, collapse, roll. This activity teaches children how to fall in a relaxed fashion so they can more easily avoid injury when they fall in running games.

5. Can you be a bag of potatoes falling to the ground? Show me how a feather would look falling to the ground. Did you feel differently? How did your shape, speed, and force change?

   Can you be water dripping out of a faucet? a leaf floating to the ground? water pouring out of a pitcher? an ice-cream cone melting? snow falling? Can you fall on a giant sponge? Can you be a spaceship landing on the moon?

Discuss the different feelings the children experienced, the weight of their objects, the amounts of force they used, and the speeds with which they fell.

What can you deduce from these experiments? [The heavier the object, the greater the force of attraction.]

6. How would you move if you were on the moon? You can jump six times as high on the moon as you can on earth, and you weigh much less. Pretend you are on the moon. Move around the room skipping, hopping, leaping, jumping, running, galloping, and walking. Remember the pull of gravity is much less on the moon than on the earth. You feel very, very light and move with a great deal of spring and bounce. Let us watch half the room at a time to see how people on the moon might move.

Matter

1. What is the arrangement of molecules in a gas? [The molecules are spaced far apart.] Each person be a molecule. Use all the space in the room to move about. Move on different levels and in different directions. Try some different molecule shapes as you move as a gas molecule.

2. What is the arrangement of molecules in a liquid? [Molecules are spaced closer together than they are in a gas.] Each individual be a molecule and show me the spatial arrangement of molecules in milk. Move around the room but use only one-half of the space we have available. *(Point out the half you want the students to use.)* Do you feel other molecules are closer to you than they were when you were an oxygen molecule?

3. What is the arrangement of molecules in a solid? [Molecules are spaced very close together.] Each individual be a molecule and show me the spatial arrangement of molecules in rock. This time we will only use one-eighth of the space in our room. What happens to your movement in this small space? [Range of movement decreases and molecules bump against each other.]

4. *(Divide the class into groups.)* Can each group show me the transformation of ice into water and then into water vapor? Each individual in your group be a molecule and all together demonstrate the spatial arrangement of molecules in the solid,

*Can you show the arrangement of molecules in a solid? in a liquid? in a
gas?* The students in the foreground are forming a solid; the students in
the center, a liquid; and the students in the background, a gas.
("Matter," Problems 1, 2, 3)

liquid, and gas. When everyone is ready, we will watch each
group and discuss the different ways this problem was solved.

5. Let's work together to form the atoms of some of the
   elements. Can you find a partner and form a hydrogen atom?
   (See Diagram 13.) I should see one electron circling one
   proton. Electrons have a negative charge and protons a positive
   charge. Can you show this somehow through your shape or
   movement?

   Can you work with two other pairs of people to form a helium
   atom? *(See Diagram 14.)* A helium atom has two electrons
   circling two protons, and it also has two neutrons in its
   nucleus. Neutrons are neutral electrically. You remember from
   working with magnets that like charges repel each other.
   Without the neutrons the protons would fly away from one

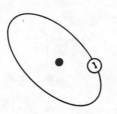

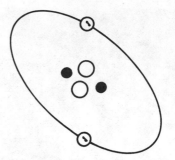

Diagram 13. A hydrogen atom has one electron circling a proton. ("Matter," Problem 5)

Diagram 14. A helium atom has two neutrons holding two protons in its nucleus which is circled by two electrons. ("Matter," Problem 5)

another. Can you show through movement the holding quality of the neutrons upon the protons?

6. If we add one more proton to the nucleus of an atom to make three, we would normally find four neutrons. This combination gives us a solid—the metal lithium—instead of a gas. Can you form a lithium atom in your group? *(See Diagram 15.)* You will need four neutrons holding three protons, circled by three electrons—two in the first orbit and one in the second orbit. Let's look at each group and discuss the different solutions we see.

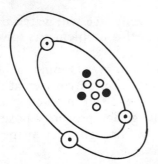

Diagram 15. A lithium atom has four neutrons holding three protons, circled by three electrons—two in the first orbit and one in the second orbit. ("Matter," Problem 6)

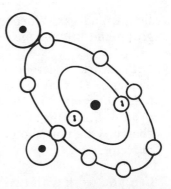

Diagram 16. A water molecule is composed of two hydrogen atoms and one oxygen atom. ("Matter," Problem 8)

7. What does the weight of an atom tell us? [How many protons and how many neutrons the atom has.] Normally, how many electrons does an atom have? [An atom normally has as many electrons revolving about the nucleus as it has protons in the nucleus.]

Let's form several atoms. Can we form a beryllium atom? If the atomic weight is nine, how many protons will we need? [Four.] How many neutrons? [Five.] How many electrons? [Four.]

Try forming as many atoms as possible. With the larger atoms you might leave off the electrons.

8. Let's try forming a molecule of water. *(See Diagram 16.)* The symbol for water is H_2O. How many hydrogen atoms will we need? [Two.] How many oxygen atoms will we need? [One.] Water is formed from the combustion of the hydrogen and oxygen gases. Two hydrogen atoms are attracted to an oxygen atom. The oxygen atom traps the two hydrogen atoms and

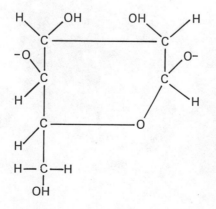

Diagram 17. The structural formula of a common molecule found in wood—$C_6H_{10}O_5$. ("Matter," Problem 9)

forms the molecule H_2O. Can you describe this process through movement? Your final molecule should look like the one I have drawn on the board. *(Try forming other simple molecules.)*

9. I have drawn on the board the structural formula for the most common type of molecule found in wood, $C_6H_{10}O_5$. *(See Diagram 17.)* Can the class work together to recreate the structural formula of this molecule? If you are a hydrogen atom form an *H* with your body. Make a *C* for a carbon atom and an *O* for an oxygen atom. How many carbon atoms will we need? [Six.] How many hydrogen atoms? [Ten.] How many oxygen atoms? [Five.] Can you think of a way to attach the atoms to each other as they are diagrammed in the picture on the board?

Try making other structural formulas of molecules such as methane (CH_4), ethane (C_2H_6), hydrazine (NH_2NH_2), and rubber (C_5H_8).

Can you form a methane molecule (CH_4)? The student in the center is the carbon atom. The four surrounding students represent the hydrogen atoms. *("Matter," Problem 9)*

10. Let's describe a chemical reaction through movement. Water and sulfur trioxide combine to form hydrogen sulfate (sulfuric acid, $H_2O + SO_3 = H_2SO_4$). We need three people to form the water molecules and four people to form the sulfur trioxide molecule. When they combine, they will have to restructure themselves to form a new molecule—hydrogen sulfate. Let's try several other chemical reactions.

PART IV

SOCIAL STUDIES PROBLEMS

Natural Resources

Transportation

Cultures

Occupations

HOLIDAYS

GOVERNMENT

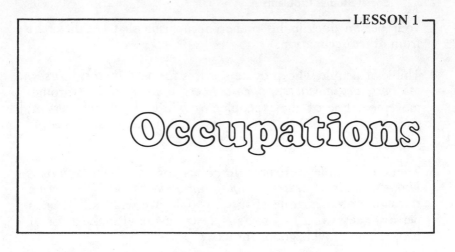

Occupations

The problems in this chapter can be solved with the class as a whole or with small groups.

1. Who are people in our community that help us? I will write a list of helpers on the board as you name them. *(Police, letter carriers, doctors, teachers, electricians, delivery people, parents, sisters, brothers, store clerks, newspaper carriers, etc.).* Pick one of these helpers and describe the helper through movement. Think of the special thing your helper does and include that in your movement. Does your helper ever do his or her work on a different level? Try your actions sitting, standing, or lying down. Let's look at some of the helpers being described. First, let's try to guess who they are, and then let's decide on which level they do most of their work.

2. Who are people in other communities that help us? *(This depends on the type of community you live in—urban or rural. Some answers may be: ranchers, farmers, field hands, scientists, construction workers, bakers, soldiers, judges, etc.)* Can you think of the special things each of these people do? Pick one person and describe his or her occupation through movement. Let's try to guess each occupation being described.

3. Can we make a list of people who help us travel near and far? *(Possible answers are: bus and cab drivers and all the different people associated with trains, planes, and boats.)* Choose one occupation and show through movement three different things

your person does in his or her occupation that are different from other occupations.

4. Think of people who provide services for us. *(Doctors, nurses, teachers, dry cleaners, police officers, etc.).* Describe through movement one of these people. We will look at each person, guess who he or she is describing, and make a list of people who serve us.

5. Think of people who provide goods for us. *(Manufacturers, farmers, bakers, crafts people, lumberjacks, etc.)* Describe through movement one of those people. We will look at each person, guess who he or she is describing, and make a list of people who provide goods for us.

6. Are there jobs in the United States that do not exist in other countries? Does every country have astronauts, presidents, cowboys, ski instructors, or coal miners? Can you think of any occupations that cannot be found in every country in the world? Describe one through movement. We will make a list of

Can you describe through movement people who provide services for us? These children are describing police officers directing traffic. ("Occupations," Problem 4)

Who is another person who provides a service for us? Here is a doctor listening to a patient's heart. ("Occupations," Problem 4)

the occupations you portray and discuss what countries do not offer these jobs and why. We will also discuss countries that do offer the same jobs.

7. Are there countries in the world where there are jobs that do not exist in the United States? Do we have camel drivers, gondola drivers, or cricket players? Can you think of jobs found in other countries but not in the United States? If you cannot think of a job, describe one of the jobs I mentioned. If you can think of another job, describe the job through movement. We will try to guess it and discuss why it does not exist in the United States. *(Rickshaw drivers, rice, coffee, and olive growers, queens, kings, and premiers are some examples of jobs found elsewhere.)*

8. Are there any jobs that are common to all countries? Think of one and describe it through movement. We will make a list of the jobs described and discuss the importance of them. *(Possible solutions are: parents, food gatherers or providers, weapon and/or tool makers, doctors or healers, and shelter builders.)*

9. Were there occupations in our ancestors' time that we no longer see today or that have changed somehow? *(Pony express riders, stagecoach drivers, steamboat pilots, slaves,*

bounty hunters, and buffalo hunters are possible answers.) Think of one and describe the occupation through movement. Then we will guess it and discuss the reason it has changed or no longer exists.

10. Are there occupations today that were not available two hundred years ago? *(Pilots, astronauts, electricians, motorized vehicle drivers, train engineers, telephone operators, recording artists, telegraph operators, and plumbers are possible answers.)* Choose one to describe through movement. After we guess the ones shown, we will try to think of others you might have overlooked.

11. Can you think of any occupation that does not exist today but might be needed in the future? *(Occupations related to public space travel, new machinery or inventions, handling or producing new resources or new modes of transportation, and new positions in government are possible answers.)* Can you think of any occupations that might become obsolete in one hundred years? Choose one possible future occupation and one possible obsolete occupation to describe through movement. Be prepared to discuss the reasons behind your choices.

12. Can you think of an occupation for every letter of the alphabet? *(This is possible.)* As I go through the alphabet, think of an occupation beginning with each letter and describe the occupation through movement. We will stop after each letter and name the occupations we see. If you cannot think of an occupation for a certain letter, wait until I have named one and then describe the occupation in your own way.

    You may want to do half the alphabet one day and the other half the next day. Small groups can be assigned several letters of the alphabet that can be worked on simultaneously in the groups.

13. Can people have more than one occupation? Who do you know who has more than one occupation? Think of all the occupations your person has and describe each one through movement for the class. We will discuss the various occupations people have and their significance.

Transportation

1. Can you name some means of transportation—ways that we get from one place to another? Choose one of the ideas mentioned and describe your means of transportation through movement. Before you begin to move, think of your vehicle's size, shape, speed, and color. Try to use all these elements in your movement. Remember, you are not the driver of your vehicle, you *are* the vehicle. We will look at the solutions and discuss the different ways people solved the problem.

2. Can you think of transportation that is found mainly in a city or town? *(Subways, monorails, escalators, police cars, ambulances, street cleaners, trolley cars, taxis, limousines are possible answers.)* Describe one kind of city transportation through movement.

   What transportation do you find mainly on farms or ranches? *(Horses, tractors, hay wagons, grain harvesters, and pick-up trucks are possible answers.)* Choose one kind of country transportation to describe through movement.

   Now find a partner. One of you describe a kind of transportation found mainly in the city, and the other describe a kind of transportation found mainly in the country. We will watch each pair as they do their movements at the same time. Can you guess what they are describing, which belongs in the city and which in the country, and why?

3. Can you think of transportation that is found on water?

Everyone choose one form of transportation we have discussed and describe it through movement. ("Transportation," Problem 1)

Describe a type of water transportation through movement. Let's make a list of the types being shown. Can you think of any other vehicles that move on water? Describe another water vehicle through movement. Choose one that is very different from your first so that you will have to change shape, size, level, and speed. Let's look at these second choices and add them to our water transportation list.

4. What are some types of transportation that travel in the sky? Instead of just flying around the room like a plane, can you show me a particular type of aircraft? Are you large or small, slow or fast? Do you have propellers, jets, rockets? Do you carry passengers or cargo? Try to make your shape and movement special so that we can tell what type of plane you are.

What are some unusual types of air transportation? *(Balloons, hang gliders, blimps, being shot out of a cannon, antique airplanes, and parachutes are possible answers.)* Can you describe one of these unusual methods of air travel? Let's look at the solutions and guess the answers. Can you think of types of aircraft that can land on water *and* ground? *(Seaplanes, hovercraft, and space capsules are possible solutions.)*

5. Many types of transportation are run by motors. Can you think of types of transportation that do not have motors to make them run? [Animals transport us, and we transport ourselves on motorless vehicles.] Can you name animals that people use for transportation? Think of animals in other countries besides our own. Do you know what children ride in the deserts of Africa or on the roads in India or in the snow in Northern Canada? Let's discuss many forms of animal transportation.

Now choose one that interests you to describe through movement. You might be the animal, the driver, the rider, or the vehicle being pulled by the animal. We will guess the solutions when everyone is ready.

These are some additional questions you might want to discuss: what animals are not used for transportation and why; why are the animals used chosen to do the tasks they do?

6. Besides animals, we have other kinds of motorless transportation. Can you think of any? *(Sleds, skates, cycles of all kinds, pogo sticks, wagons, skis, rowboats, sailboats, gliders, rafts, inner tubes, and stilts are possible answers.)* Describe one kind through movement. Let's guess the solutions and discuss their usefulness for long or short trips.

7. Let's name different countries we have studied. Can you think of transportation used in these countries that usually is not used in the United States? *(Possible answers are: rickshaw-Japan; troika-Russia; camel-Africa; elephant-India; double-decker bus-England; dog sled-Northern Canada; burro-Mexico; palanquin or sultan's chair-Far East.)*

Let's go through the list we have made and describe the kinds of transportation through movement. You will need to work with one or two friends to describe some of the kinds.

Have all the children describe all of the foreign types of transportation. Some of these types of transportation are unfamiliar to the children, and the names and shapes will be better remembered if they are described through movement.

8. Can you describe through movement transportation used in other countries that is also used in the United States? Let's look at your solutions and make a list of kinds of transportation shared by many countries. Do all countries in the world use the kinds of transportation on our list? Why not? *(Economic reasons, lack of skills and resources to make transportation, lack of need, and not functional for terrain or climate are some possible answers.)*

9. Can you name and describe through movement some ways that boys and girls travel to school in other countries? *(Cars, buses, walking, bicycles, boats, skates, skis, burros, elephants, camels, horses, scooters are possible answers.)* After we have guessed everyone's transportation let's make a list and match the countries to the transportation.

10. Can you describe through movement transportation our ancestors used that is not as commonly used today? *(The steamboat, travois, stagecoach, raft, horse-and-buggy, covered wagon, oxen-drawn vehicles, frigate, and schooner are possible answers.)*

Who can show us kinds of transportation used today that was not available two hundred years ago? one hundred years ago? fifty years ago?

Can you design a vehicle that might be needed fifty years from now but is not available today? You may work with friends or by yourself. When you have your plans down on paper, transcribe your design into movement for the class. Your futuristic vehicle should have a name and purpose.

11. Instead of describing a vehicle through movement, describe the actions of a driver of a certain vehicle. How does the driver of a dog sled handle the dog team? What level is he or she on when driving? What things does a dog sled driver hold? Show

me. How does a rickshaw driver handle a rickshaw? Where does he stand in relationship to the vehicle? What level is a rickshaw driver on? Show me. How does a rower handle a boat? What does a rower hold? What level is a rower on? Show me. How does a person in a kayak move? Show me. How does a ship's captain drive a ship? Show me the level the captain works at and the actions of his or her arms. How does a bicyclist handle a bicycle? What is different about a unicyclist? What is different about a motorcyclist? Can you show me?

Continue in this fashion using other vehicles. You may need to have a discussion of the vehicles or show pictures before the children move.

12. Can all modes of transportation move in different directions? Are there any that cannot move backwards? [Some animals, planes, bicycles.] Think of one and show me through movement. Can you think of any more?

Can you think of a vehicle that can move sideways? *(A helicopter, canoe, rowboat, and raft are possible answers.)* Choose one we named and show it moving sideways. Be sure you describe its shape, size, and speed.

Now choose a vehicle that can move in more than one direction and describe its movements, shape, size, and speed as it goes in different directions. Can it go the same speed in all directions? *(For example, a car can go backwards as fast as it can go forwards but a horse cannot. The answer will vary according to the transportation.)*

13. *(Divide the class into groups.)* I am going to give each group a card with a location written on it. Think of one kind of transportation found in your location and work together to describe the size, shape, movements, directions, and speeds of your transportation. When everyone is ready, we will look at the groups' solutions and discuss what we see.

Give locations such as: on land; on water; under water; in the air; in the mountains; in the desert; in cities; on farms; in Russia; in India; in South America; in the Far East; in Africa, etc.

Can your group make a form of transportation that travels in space? These children are creating a rocket. ("Transportation," Problem 13)

14. Can you think of funny, imaginary kinds of transportation? What could a mouse ride in? [A cheese-mobile.] What could a worm drive? [An apple-cycle.] Make up imaginary means of transportation. Describe your transportation through movement, and we will try to guess what kind of person or animal could drive or ride in it.

Show the children Richard Scarry's book Cars and Trucks and Things That Go *for more ideas.*

Groups in the Community

1. What is the name of the group that you were born into? [The family.] Show me how many members belong to your family group by making the shape of the number with your body. How many adults are in your family? How many children? How many parents? sisters? brothers? grandmothers? grandfathers? uncles? aunts? cousins? nieces? nephews? babies? pets? Does anyone have someone else in his or her family group that I did not mention? Tell us about that person.

    Variation: Have children touch body parts to the floor or do actions to show the numbers.

2. I am going to ask you some true and false questions about family groups. If the answer is true, make the shape of a *T* with your body. If the answer is false, make the shape of an *F*.
    a. All family groups have the same number of people in them. [F]
    b. The members of your family can live apart and still belong to your family. [T]
    c. A family must have pets before they can be a family. [F]
    d. Everybody has a family. [F]

    Continue with other questions relating to the family unit. Be sensitive to issues such as adoption, divorce, and death of a family member. Discuss each statement before going on to the next one.

3. People in groups work together to help one another. Can you

219

describe through movement one thing parents do to help their children? One thing sisters and brothers do to help each other? One thing children do to help their parents? Let's look at the solutions and discuss the ways in which families help each other.

Are there other ways of helping that were not shown? Can you show me those now? Did we name some of the ways in which your own family members help each other? Did you get some new ideas to share with your family tonight?

4. You belong to a family group. What other groups do you belong to? Make a list of all the groups you belong to. *(Or draw a picture of each group.)* Choose one group to portray through movement. We will watch each person in the class describe his or her group. Guess the name of the group and check your list. Do you also belong to that group?

   Possible groups are: scouts, play groups, school class, teams, hobby groups, orchestra group.

5. *(Divide the class into groups.)* Each group think of a type of group that adults belong to. Describe that group through movement. Use levels, locomotor and nonlocomotor movement, force, and shape to describe your group accurately. We will guess and discuss the different groups shown.

   Possible groups are: explorers, astronauts, doctors, bridge club, sailors, soldiers, mounted police, professional sports teams, geologists, coal miners, senate, etc. You may want to assign categories.

Problems 6, 7, and 8 deal with the organization of groups.

6. How are groups organized? How do leaders emerge? How do people get along in groups? Let's do some exercises that will help us find these answers. Walk around the room. When I give the signal, form four straight lines standing shoulder-to-shoulder. That took a while. Could you do it faster? Walk around again. On the signal, form four straight lines standing shoulder-to-shoulder. That was faster. What are some things you can do to get organized quickly? [Let people in line;

How quickly can you form four lines that are fairly equal in length? ("Groups in the Community," Problem 6)

people could say *1st, 2nd, 3rd, 4th* and raise their hands to indicate line leaders; or if you are standing alone, you could move quickly to a formed line.]

Repeat the exercise several times until four lines are formed in a matter of seconds. Then try four equal lines; two lines with people standing back to stomach in the lines; one line; five lines, etc.

7. Walk around the room on different levels. When I give the signal, form one large circle with everyone evenly spaced on it. Walk around again and on the signal form two circles; three circles; one big circle and one small circle; a figure eight; a square; a triangle; a rectangle.

Repeat each formation several times until the students can get into the formation quickly and without pushing and shoving. Furthermore, repeat the activity occasionally throughout the year, discussing changes in organization and leadership. It is

*interesting to note the different strategies that evolve from the
repetition of this problem.*

8. How many different ways can we divide the class into four
    groups? We will try each suggestion.

    *Possible suggestions are: count off by fours or four colors,
    animals, etc.; divide by boys and girls and then divide the boys
    in half and the girls in half; get into four equal lines as quickly
    as possible; choose four squad leaders and have them choose
    teams; if the class has four rows of seats, use those four
    groups.*

    Which method of grouping did you like the most? Why?
    (Answers will vary.) Which method did you like the least?
    Why? Which method was the slowest? Which method was the
    fastest? Should we choose one method to use always? What is
    the benefit of having several methods to choose from? Why
    would some methods work better than others for certain
    activities? How do other groups get members? *(Elections, skill,
    money, common goals are possible answers.)*

    Try other number groupings such as two, three, ten, and five.

9. *(Divide the class into groups.)* Do groups working together
    always agree? Can you think of groups in our community that
    sometimes disagree? *(Students and teachers, children and
    parents, employers and employees, teammates and umpires or
    referees are possible answers.)*

    What are larger groups that sometimes disagree? *(Govern-
    ments, political parties, unions, judicial courts, religious groups
    are possible answers.)*

    I am going to give each group a card with a situation written
    on it. Describe your situation clearly through movement.

    Possible situations are the following:
    a. *Two groups arguing; they cannot come to an agreement
        but depart peaceably.*
    b. *Two groups arguing; they cannot come to an agreement
        and a mock battle ensues.*

c. *Two groups arguing; they reach agreement and depart together.*
d. *Two groups arguing; no agreement is reached but several members of the groups switch sides.*
e. *Two groups arguing; another person enters, talks to each group and brings them together.*
f. *Same as situation e, except that the groups do not come together.*
g. *Two groups arguing as a third group watches; the two groups do not reach agreement, and members of the third group join the first and second groups until only two groups remain.*
h. *Two groups arguing; a third group is formed by members of the first two groups.*

After the situations have been shown, discuss them and try to relate them to actual events in history or everyday life.

Can you think of a real life situation to match situation *a*? [A political debate.]   to match situation *b*? [Revolutionary War.] situations *e* and *f*? [Government diplomatic meetings.]

Customs and Cultures

1. Customs are the ways people in a group have done things for many, many years. Can you show me through movement a custom that your family has at mealtimes? Let's look at the solutions when everyone is ready and discuss the different customs being shown. *(Saying grace, using silverware, eating at a table, children clearing dishes are possible solutions.)*

   Do you think everyone in the world has the same customs at mealtime that you do? Can you think of another country where the customs may be different? If you can, show me through movement a custom from another country related to eating. *(Eating with chopsticks or hands, children drinking wine instead of milk, eating around a fire instead of a table are possible solutions.)* Let's look at some of the customs you thought of and some pictures that I have and discuss what we see. Why do you think people have different customs about eating? How did the customs develop?

2. What are some ways of showing respect? Can you show me through movement? *(Shaking hands, taking off a hat inside the house, standing when an older person enters, sending thank-you notes for gifts, opening the door for a friend, listening to someone else are possible solutions.)* Let's look at your solutions and discuss them.

   Can you find out how children in other countries show respect?

How do children in other countries say "Thank you"? In Japan they bow; in India they bow their heads over their hands in a prayer position; and in England they curtsy. ("Customs and Cultures," Problem 2)

3. Can you show me customs you have concerning holidays? What are some customs related to Halloween? Show me through movement. Show me some customs related to Thanksgiving; Fourth of July; Valentine's Day; New Year's Day; Christmas. Does everyone in the United States celebrate these holidays?

   What are other holidays celebrated in this country? *(Hanukkah, Chinese New Year, St. Patrick's Day are possible answers.)* Where did these holidays originate? Why do we celebrate them in this country?

   Do children in other countries celebrate any of the same holidays you do? Find out which holidays you share with other countries and which holidays you do not share. Find out the reasons behind your answers. Find out the customs surrounding holidays in other countries and describe these customs through movement for your friends.

4. A cultural trait is a part of a way of life that is learned. Can you describe through movement a cultural trait you share with a friend? *(Going to school, reading, writing, playing sports, riding a bicycle are possible answers.)* Let's look at the solutions when everyone is ready and make a list of the cultural traits being shown.

   Can you think of another cultural trait and describe it through movement? We will add it to our list. How did you learn the cultural traits on our list? [From teachers, parents, friends, TV, making mistakes, watching others.]

5. Can you describe through movement some cultural traits of your parents that you will learn some day? *(Driving a car, different work skills, being a parent are possible solutions.)* Let's discuss the traits being shown.

6. Do children in other cultures have the same traits you do? Can you describe through movement some cultural traits of Eskimo children? Japanese children? African children? *(Use the cultures you have studied in class.)*

7. Can cultural traits ever be changed? Can you show me one new cultural trait you would learn if you moved from Texas to Alaska—from a hot, sunny state to a cold, snowy state? *(Skiing, skating, ice fishing, sledding are possible answers.)*

   Why would you learn a new trait? [So you could better adapt to your new environment.] Would you have to change all your cultural traits? Can you describe through movement cultural traits that might be the same in both environments? *(Going to school, reading, writing are possible solutions.)*

8. Can you describe through movement some ways the Pilgrims had to adapt to their new environment? What new cultural traits did they learn? *(New foods, new jobs, new houses, new games are possible solutions.)* How did they learn these traits? [From the Indians and through trial and error.] Can you describe through movement ways in which other cultures have

Can you catch the fish's tail? This is a game children play in China. ("Customs and Cultures," Problem 9)

had to learn new cultural traits? *(Discuss the cultures you have been studying.)*

9. *Teach games from the different cultures you are studying. Compare and contrast them to games in our culture. For the rules of games from foreign countries see* ICHPER Book of Worldwide Games and Dances; Learning About Human Behavior: Through Active Games, *Bryant Cratty; and other general elementary physical education books. Have the children invent their own games after learning several new ones.*

10. *Teach folk dances from different cultures you are studying, including our own. Find out the history behind the dance. Bring in pictures of costumes or authentic costumes. Research the background of your students' parents. One of them may be able to teach a dance. See the Bibliography in this book for records and books dealing with folk dances. Have the children create new steps or entire folk dances to music from other lands.*

Holidays

Halloween

1. What does Halloween celebrate? [End of summer, beginning of winter, and remembrances of the dead.] Can you show me through movement some symbols of Halloween? *(Jack-o-lantern, cat, witch, ghost, skeleton are possible solutions.)* Let's look at the different solutions and discuss the meanings behind the symbols.

2. *(Divide the class into groups.)* Each group think of a Halloween activity to describe through movement for the rest of the class. *(Or assign activities.)* We will guess the activities and discuss their origins.

   Some Halloween customs and their origins are: jack-o-lanterns came from Ireland; trick-or-treating came from Ireland and is also practiced in England, France, and Ireland. Other activities might include bobbing for apples, husking bees, and ghost-story telling.

3. Can you find Halloween customs from other countries and describe them through movement?

4. What emotions do you express on Halloween? Choose one to describe through movement. Use your whole body. Move in different directions. Can you show me another emotion? Let's divide the class in half. Each half show the emotions you go through on Halloween. Let's make a list of the emotions and

discuss the reasons for all these different feelings. *(Terror, excitement, mystery, fantasy, and exhilaration are possible solutions.)*

5. *(Divide the class into groups.)* Each group design a jack-o-lantern. Use levels, shapes, and pathways to make your jack-o-lantern interesting. We will look at each group when everyone is ready. *(The younger children can form jack-o-lanterns with a partner or by themselves.)*

6. I am going to play some mysterious, spooky music. *(Danse Macabre is a good piece. See Bibliography.)* Pretend you are in a haunted house or graveyard on Halloween night. Every time you hear a strange noise, change your focus, run toward or away from the noise, and change your level. Move quickly, then slowly. When I give the signal, change from a person to a Halloween symbol. Move about in the shape and with the movements that match your symbol. We will divide the class in half and watch the Halloween dances you created.

As the music is playing, move about the room and occasionally moan, hoot, or cackle. The children should focus on you, wherever you are, when you make a noise. This is a good listening exercise.

7. *(Have the children design Halloween masks out of paper bags. Do not cut holes for eyes.)* Put on your masks and move slowly in your own space. Try balancing on one leg; twisting; bouncing up and down; turning in a circle; swaying back and forth. Now try moving through space. When I see someone about to bump into something, I will clap my hands. That means stop! Try changing levels and directions. How does it feel to have your sense of sight taken away?

Thanksgiving

8. Can you think of a holiday in the fall that we celebrate? [Thanksgiving.] Show me through movement the first thing that comes into your mind about Thanksgiving. Let's look at all the solutions and make a list of Thanksgiving things. Can you think of any more? Show me through movement.

9. Why do we celebrate Thanksgiving? Let's recreate the first Thanksgiving. What characters do we need? What objects or props do we need? Do you think some of you could make the shapes of some of the objects? *(Tables, chairs, turkeys, trees are possible solutions.)* Who invited whom to dinner? What did they eat? What games did they play? Do you know what the weather was like? Let's put everything together to produce a silent film of the first Thanksgiving.

   With older children, the class may be divided in half. Each half can watch the recreation of the first Thanksgiving by the other half. Both silent films can be compared and discussed in positive terms.

10. What are some of the activities we do on Thanksgiving today? Can you show me through movement? Can you think of an activity that is done on a different level? Show me. Let's look at some of the activities and discuss them. Do all of you do the same activities? [Probably not.] Is there one activity that you all do that is the same? [Perhaps eating.] Let's share some of our family Thanksgiving customs with each other. Who would like to show us something special you do at your house on Thanksgiving? The rest of us will join in. *(Continue sharing customs.)*

11. What are some emotions you experience on Thanksgiving Day? Express one of those feelings through movement. Use your whole body. Use different levels and directions. *(Discuss the emotions expressed.)*

   Do you have any other feelings on Thanksgiving Day? If you do, show me. Let's share our feelings and our reasons behind these feelings with each other.

   Some responses might be: excitement, joy, thankfulness, peacefulness, happiness. Some children may express sadness or loneliness if their families are not together. This activity could provide the opportunity to release these feelings.

12. Do other countries celebrate Thanksgiving Day? Why not? Do you think other countries have a holiday that is similar to our Thanksgiving? Let's find out and then show some of the

activities boys and girls in other countries do on their "thanksgiving" days.

Christmas

13. What comes to mind when I say Christmas? Show me one thing. Show me another; another; and another. Show me something that doesn't move. Now show me something that does move. Let's make a list of Christmas things.

14. Each one of you think of a present you would like to receive on Christmas. Make the shape, size, and movement, if any, of your present. We will look at the presents when everyone is ready and guess what they are.

Now think of a present you would like to give to someone. Show the present through movement, and we will make a list of these presents.

You may want to have the children write their own lists for practice in vocabulary and spelling skills.

15. What does Christmas celebrate? Could we reenact the first Christmas? What characters do we need? What is the setting? What is the weather like? What objects or animals are needed?

Assign characters, discuss the plot, and then proceed with the play. Older children can be divided into groups to work on their own versions of the story. After the plays are performed, the different versions can be discussed. Some groups may prefer to do silent versions while others would rather use words.

16. What are some of the activities you do to prepare for Christmas Day? Can you show me? What are some of the activities you do *on* Christmas Day? Show me. Does everyone in the class do the same things? Do you do them at the same time? Let's share some of our family customs with each other.

17. Do people in other countries celebrate Christmas? What people in what countries celebrate Christmas? Do they celebrate Christmas the same way we do? Can you find out different

Christmas customs from other lands to describe through movement? If you find one, you can teach it to the class.

In the process of this research children may discover where some of our customs originated: caroling and plum pudding from England; Christmas trees from Germany; kissing under mistletoe from Scandinavia; Santa Claus from Holland. Customs in other lands include: leaving grain in wooden shoes for Santa's reindeer on December 6-Holland; carrying a large wooden star called a "Steaua" while caroling-Romania; breaking a piñata-Mexico; making a Ceppo, a wooden tree with shelves for toys-Italy; as evening stars appear, serving a dinner that consists of twelve courses for the twelve apostles-Poland; making layettes for expectant friends and poor mothers on Christmas Eve-France; giving extra food to the birds and animals-Scandinavia.

18. *(Divide the class into groups.)* Each group think of a Christmas symbol. *(Or assign symbols such as wreath, holly, star, tree, bell, candle.)* Work together to form one symbol to show to the class. Can you think of three different ways to depict your Christmas symbol? When everyone is ready, we will look at the three solutions of each group and guess the symbol.

19. Can you make up a riddle about Christmas? If you can, write it down and give it to a friend. Let your friend show you the answer through movement. Here is a riddle to get you started:

> Tall and green;
> On top a star.
> Presents below
> from near and far.
> What am I? [Christmas tree.]

20. What emotions do you express around Christmas time? Show me, using your whole body. Use the qualities of force to show me your different feelings. What are your reasons for feeling this way?

Hanukkah

21. Does everyone in the United States celebrate Christmas? What is a winter holiday that Jewish children enjoy? [Hanukkah,

Diagram 18. Menorah. ("Holidays," Problem 21)

Festival of Lights.] Can you get together with some friends and show me the symbol of Hanukkah? [The menorah, a candelabrum with nine candles.] Do people in other countries celebrate Hanukkah? [Jews all over the world celebrate this holiday.]

22. Show me how many days Hanukkah lasts by touching the correct number of body parts to the floor; by jumping the number of days; by making the number with your body. [Eight days.]

23. What happens each night of Hanukkah? Show me one thing. [Each night a candle on the menorah is lit. The center candle is used to light the others.] Show me another happening. [A present is opened each night of Hanukkah.]

24. What emotions are associated with Hanukkah? Can you show me through movement? *(Joy, pride, happiness are possible emotions.)* Let's watch each other and discuss the emotions we see and the reasons behind the emotions.

25. *Teach the students dreidel games and songs. The dreidel is a four-sided top played with during Hanukkah. Games and songs may be found in* The Book of Festival Holidays *by Marguerite Ickis.*

St. Valentine's Day

26. Do you know how Valentine's Day originated? St. Valentine was a young Roman who was killed because he would not give up Christianity. He died in A.D. 270 on February 14. Legend says that he left a farewell note for the jailer's daughter signed, "From your Valentine." Can you think of signs and symbols connected with Valentine's Day that may have come from the Romans? Describe a symbol through movement. *(Hearts, roses, cupids, violets are possible answers.)* Let's look at the solutions and discuss the meanings behind the symbols.

27. Can you find out where else Valentine's Day is celebrated in the world and describe some of the different customs through movement?

    In England children eat valentine buns containing currants and plums, and suitors leave baskets of gifts on their lovers' doorsteps. In Italy, an unmarried girl gets up very early, watching for the first man to pass her house; he is destined to become her husband.

28. *(Divide the class into groups.)* Can each group describe through movement some activities connected with Valentine's Day? We will guess what each group is doing when everyone is ready.

29. What emotions do you express on Valentine's Day? Show me through movement. *(Love, happiness, gaiety, disappointment, nervousness are possible solutions.)* Let's discuss the emotions you expressed and the reasons behind the emotions.

30. *(Divide the class into groups.)* Each group design a valentine using body shapes and levels. Maybe part of your valentine will move. When your valentine is ready, present it to the class. We will look at each human valentine and discuss all its different parts.

31. Make up a moving valentine for a friend. Instead of writing down your valentine sentiments, describe them through movement. If you do not want to create a valentine for a classmate,

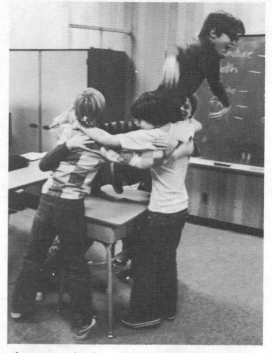

Show me a summer holiday through movement. These children are showing a bursting firecracker to represent the Fourth of July. ("Holidays," Problem 32)

Can you portray a holiday that comes in the spring? These children are portraying the traditional Easter bunny. ("Holidays," Problem 32)

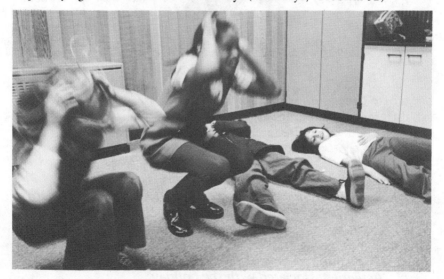

Do each one of us have our own special holiday? These children are the candles and cake representing a birthday. ("Holidays," Problem 32)

create one for someone at home. Use levels, directions, different locomotor movements, and qualities of force to make your valentine interesting and meaningful.

Other Holidays

32. *Discuss other holidays, including birthdays and holidays from other countries. Relate the ideas from the previous problems to these holidays, discussing and describing the following through movement:*
   a. Origin and meaning of the holiday;
   b. Activities associated with the holiday;
   c. Symbols;

d. *Another country's customs;*
e. *Emotions associated with the holiday; and*
f. *Stories and poems related to the holiday.*

See the books in the Bibliography on holidays.

Physical Environment

Problems 1-5 explore climate and how it effects our environment. Have the children answer all your questions through movement.

1. There are nine major types of climate. As I ask you questions about the climates, try to answer the questions through movement. The type of climate found most often near the equator is called *rainy tropical*. What types of weather do you think people in this climate experience? Can you show me through movement? That's right. There is rainfall all year round and the temperature is hot year round.

    Can you show me what kind of countryside you might see there? Would there be trees and plants or sandy deserts? Would you have to wear overcoats and mittens or cool summer clothes? Would your houses need furnaces or fans? Would you more likely travel by boat or sled? Would you serve hot soup or cold drinks to your friends? Would your parents earn a living by ice fishing or farming? Would you see monkeys or polar bears in this climate? Do you live in this type of climate? Are the objects you made with your body part of your environment? *(Some of them are. Discuss the similarities. Explore the* wet and dry tropical *climate in a similar fashion.)*

2. Another type of climate is called *semiarid*. Arid means dry. What do you think the first two climates have that this climate doesn't have? That is correct. There is very little rainfall in this climate. The days are hot but the nights are cold. Parts of Nebraska, Kansas, Colorado, Washington, Wyoming, and

Montana have a semiarid climate. What do people use in this climate for building materials? [Rock, bricks, lumber.] Do you think anyone would use bamboo? Would people have furnaces or fans in their houses? [They might have both.] If you wanted to be a farmer what big problem would you have to solve first? [How to get water.] Can you describe through movement some ways farmers solve this problem? *(Digging irrigation ditches, pumping water, building or being windmills are possible solutions.)* Would you see monkeys and alligators or cattle and sheep in this climate? Would you travel mostly by land vehicles or boats?

Do you live in this type of environment? *(If the children do, continue.)* What else do you have in your environment that people living in the rainy tropical climate might not have?

Ask similar questions about the desert *climate including exploration of animals, plants, transportation, and housing.*

3. The *warm rainy* and the *warm rainy with dry summer* are two more types of climate. The first is more common than the second. In these two climates the summers are warm to hot and the winters are cool. With the warm rainy climate, some rain falls during all four seasons. With the warm rainy with dry summer climate, some rain falls during three seasons and the summer remains dry.

Can you find a partner to work with? One of you describe the warm rainy climate while the other describes the warm rainy with dry summer climate. We will look at the pairs and try to guess which is which.

Will you find cactus or large trees in these climates? Will you find camels or cows? All of the dry summer climates are found on sea coasts. Can you describe through movement a common occupation related to water? [Fishing.] With your partner, can you describe through movement five things that are part of these environments that are not part of a desert environment?

4. The *cold moist* climate has cold winters and warm to hot summers. There is some rain in spring and summer and snow in autumn and winter. Much of the midwestern and northeastern

United States has this type of climate. Much of the Soviet Union also has this climate. Can you describe through movement an occupation related to the land that is common in this climate? [Farming.] What kind of clothing do people living in this climate need? What are some activities that are part of a child's environment in this climate that would not be part of the desert or rainy tropical environment? *(Sledding, skiing, skating, and building snowmen are possible solutions.)* What types of transportation are found in this climate that are not found in the desert climate? What types of animals and plants are found in the cold moist climate?

5. *(Divide the class into groups.)* The *polar* climate has short, warm summers but long, cold winters. There is little rain. Many mountain ranges have a polar climate. Northern Canada and the Soviet Union also have polar climates. In your group can you describe through movement an animal found in the polar climate? a type of transportation? an occupation? a type of clothing? a type of shelter? We will look at each group and make a list of things found in this environment.

Explore the ice cap *climate in a similar fashion.*

6. *(Pictures of environments in various climates are needed for this activity.)* I am going to hold up a picture of people living in the desert. Look at the picture carefully. Can you describe through movement one thing that is in this environment that is also in your environment? Can you describe something that is different? Let's try another environment.

Continue with other environments. Discuss the similarities and differences shown in the pictures.

7. *(Divide the class into groups.)* People have to learn to adapt to their environment in order to survive. I am going to give each group a card that describes a situation where people had to adapt to a new environment. Think of the different ways the people had to adapt to the new environment. Did their transportation change? Did they have to find new ways to prepare food, clothing, and shelter? Did their occupations change? Describe the adaptations through movement. When everyone is ready, we will look at each group and discuss the

ways in which people had to adapt to a new and different environment.

Situations such as the following may be used: Pilgrims adapting to New England; Eskimos adapting to the invasion of white settlers; pioneers adapting to life in the West; Japanese adapting to life in America and vice versa; country folk adapting to life in the city; city child adapting to life on a farm; space travelers adapting to life on the moon; a child from Hawaii adapting to life in Alaska.

8. People can change the environment in ways that are harmful if they are not careful. Can you think of one way we can harm the environment? Describe your idea through movement. Can you think of another way? another? and another? Let's look at some of the ways you discovered and discuss their significance.

    Possible ways are: pollution of air, water, and land that results in the killing of fish, birds, animals, plants, and sometimes people; man-made forest fires that result in destruction of natural habitats, soil, and lumber; poor conservation methods such as planting up and down hills instead of across them, not allowing fields to lay fallow or not rotating crops, leaving hillsides bare; overpopulation that can result in lack of food, crime, etc.

    If we continue to harm the environment in these ways what will happen? Can you show me the different ways the changed environment will affect us? *(Lack of air, water, food, and building materials are possible solutions.)* What important concept has this activity taught us? [We depend on our environment for many needs. Therefore, we should value and take care of our environment.]

9. *(This activity should be done in an open area. If one is not available, see the* variation *suggested.)* Our environment not only affects our physical needs, but it also affects our emotions. Let's do an experiment to explore this concept. I will divide the class in half. Half of you will be trees and half will be forest rangers. Those who are trees decide what type of tree you are. Are you an oak, an evergreen, a bush, a stump, a

log, a weeping willow? When you have your shape in mind, find a self space in the room far away from everybody and everything and form the shape of your tree. Forest rangers move about the room as quickly as possible, counting the trees and checking them for blight. Try many different ways of moving. *(After thirty seconds, give the signal to stop.)*

Now, something mysterious has happened to the forest; it has shrunk. All the trees come over to this area. *(Mark off an area about four feet by four feet.)* Make your tree shape and freeze as in a petrified forest. Rangers again move about the forest as quickly as possible but try not to touch any trees or other rangers. *(After thirty seconds, give the signal to stop.)* Now let's repeat the activity with the rangers being trees and the trees being rangers.

(After the activity has been repeated, call the group together for a discussion.) When you were rangers what kind of movement were you able to do in the big forest? Did your movements change in the shrunken forest? How? How did you feel in the big forest? How did you feel in the shrunken forest?

How do you feel on a walk in the country? How do you feel walking in a busy city? How do you think ten people feel living in one room? Can an environment be too large besides being too small? Have you ever been in such an environment? Describe through movement this environment and how it affected you.

Variation: If this activity is done in a classroom have all the children first move around their desks and other furniture. Then push the furniture aside and explore the feelings of moving around in open space.

Natural Resources

1. The land is one of our greatest natural resources. Its soil and minerals produce many goods for us to use. Can you describe through movement foods that are products of the land? Let's look at some of the different foods the class is making and make a list of foods.

    Now, can you describe through movement clothing that comes from the land? Let's make a list from your ideas.

    What comes from the land that is used to build shelter? Describe one building material through movement. You can see by looking at our lists how valuable a resource the land is. It provides food, clothing, and shelter.

    Explore through movement the other natural resources—water, plants, animals, and people—and their uses past and present.

2. *(You will need a picture or pictures of different items found in a grocery store or you might bring actual items to class.)* You can buy all the items in this picture in a grocery store, but they come from many different natural resources. Can you describe through movement the items that come from fields which need topsoil? Let's look at the solutions and see if we agree; then I will make a list of the items in this picture that come from the soil.

    What items come from forests? from animals? from oceans? from minerals? from factories (man-made)?

After each question, make a list of the items described by the students. Discuss and explain any misconceptions.

3. Find a partner. Think of a product and the natural resource of that product. One of you make the shape of the product, and the other make the shape of the natural resource. When everyone is ready, we will look at the different pairs and guess the product and the resource.

   Variation: Divide the class into two groups. Give cards with products written or drawn on them to one group and cards with natural resources written or drawn on them to the other group. Each student describes his or her card through movement and then tries to find the person with the matching product or resource card in the opposite group.

4. How could you use a hill to take care of some of your needs? Think of one way and describe it through movement. Let's divide the class in half and look at and discuss the different solutions. How could you use the woods to meet some of your needs? How could you use a lake to meet some of your needs?

5. *(Divide the class into groups.)* I would like each group to show me five different products we get from trees. You can use furniture only once. Individuals within the group can describe different products or the group can work together to describe each product. When each group is ready, we will guess the solutions. I hope we will have discovered at least ten different products by the time all the groups have shown their solutions.

   Repeat the activity using land and animals. For water, ask for five ways we use this natural resource.

6. *(Divide the class into groups.)* I am going to assign each group a type of building or shelter. Use small groups within your large group to describe the raw materials that make up your building or shelter. When the groups are ready, we will watch the solutions and guess the materials and the type of building or shelter. *(Assign building and shelters such as: school, teepee, house, office, igloo, tent.)*

7. Does every small community in the United States contain the

Can you show me some different products we get from trees? The children on the left are describing a table and a chair, while the child on the right is portraying a tree. ("Natural Resources," Problem 5)

natural resources necessary to produce all the goods the community might need? Can you describe a product that is not produced within twenty-five miles of your house? Can you describe any other products that are not produced in your community? Are there products produced in other countries that are used in your community? Can you show me one? Let's look at the different solutions and discuss why these products are made in other countries. *(Different environments produce different goods.)*

8. *See Problem 8, "Physical Environment," for exploration of the destruction of natural resources. Along with this problem you might include historical destruction of natural resources and its consequences such as the slaughter of buffalo, destruction of soil and creation of the Dust Bowl area in the 1930s, destruction of forests by the pioneers, destruction of beaches and wildlife by modern-day oil spills, etc.*

Government

1. Can you describe through movement an American custom? I will write a list of the customs you are describing. Now describe through movement either a school rule or a home rule. I will write a list of rules you are describing. Can you think of one law to describe through movement? I will write a list of the laws you are describing. Let's look at our lists. Can you tell me the difference between a custom, a rule, and a law? [A custom is an unconscious decision based on habit and tradition. Rules and laws are conscious decisions. Rules are directions for members of a group. Law are rules for members of a community.]

2. *(Divide the class into groups.)* Laws help people in a community to live together peacefully. In your groups talk over some laws that make it easier for people to work together. Choose one law and describe it through movement. You might depict a situation in which the law is needed and used. Try to use different levels, force, and speed in your solution. We will watch each group, and hopefully, we will have a good list of helpful laws when the groups are finished.

   You may want to assign actual laws such as: obeying traffic signals; using car lights at night; not stealing, robbing, littering, or trespassing.

3. *(Divide the class into groups.)* Do laws apply to everyone or do just certain people have to obey them? What would happen if

all children with brown eyes did not have to go to school or if all people over six feet could ignore speed limits?

Decide on a group of people, as I did in my examples, who do not have to obey a certain law. You could use eye or clothes color, size, shape, names, sex, or whatever for your groupings. Divide your group in half. Through movement show one group obeying the law and the other group breaking the law. Then show the consequences of such a society. We will discuss the solutions when everyone is ready.

4. Some laws protect people and some laws protect property. Can you describe through movement something that demonstrates a law that protects people, such as a stop sign? I will write a list on the board of the things you are describing. Can you think of another thing? and another? Now try to describe, one at a time, three things that demonstrate a law that protects property, such as a fire hydrant. Let's look at each other's solutions and make a list of laws protecting property.

   Other things that demonstrate laws protecting people might be traffic lights, seat belts, speed limit signs, flame retardant sleepwear, lifeboats, motorcycle helmets, etc. Evidence of laws protecting property might be "No Trespassing" signs, "No Littering" signs, burglar alarms, locks, watchdogs, store detectives, etc.

5. *(Divide the class into groups.)* One form of government is anarchism. Anarchism is a belief that all government regulation is wrong and that public government should be destroyed. Individuals and private groups govern the affairs of a country in an anarchy. Can you imagine what would happen if everybody could make up their own rules and laws? Can each group describe one thing that might happen in an anarchy that usually does not happen in a democracy such as we have in the United States? We will discuss your solutions and the problems that arise in an anarchy when everyone is finished.

   You might want to assign situations such as incidents that might happen in schools, factories, stores or on farms, oceans, rivers, or in the air.

6. Totalitarianism is the form of government opposite that of anarchism. In a totalitarian society there are no limits on public government. Public government makes up the laws governing everything including the family, church, and club. You could not even choose what church you wanted to go to or what job you wanted to do. There would be a small group of people making all the decisions for you. Think for a minute how you would feel living under such a government. You would never be able to vote or have any say in the choices and decisions that direct your life. Describe through movement how this would make you feel. Let's watch half of the class at a time as they describe their emotions and then discuss what we saw.

7. The form of government we have in the United States is pluralism. That means that both the government through its representatives elected by the people and the people themselves regulate the affairs of the country. The particular form of pluralism practiced in the United States is democracy. The Constitution of the United States with its Bill of Rights is an important part of our democracy. I am going to divide the

What article from the Bill of Rights is this group describing? The right of citizens to refuse search of their houses without proper warrants. ("Government," Problem 7)

class into groups and give each group a card on which is written one of the liberties from the Bill of Rights. Work together in your group to describe through movement the right written on your card. We will discuss each group's solution when everyone is ready.

Variation: Have the students research and describe through movement the English Bill of Rights, the French Rights of Man, and the Canadian Bill of Rights for comparison and contrast.

The States of the Union

1. I am going to name some states of the Union. If you think the state covers a large area, make a big body shape. If you think the state covers a small area, make a small body shape. If you think the state is medium-sized, bend over so your head is on a medium level. After you make your shape, I will point to the state on the map and tell you how it ranks with the other states in size. Are you ready?

   You may want to use these states and their rankings in area: Alaska (1); Rhode Island (50); Illinois (24); Delaware (49); Connecticut (48); Texas (2); California (3).

2. *(Divide the class into groups.)* How quickly can your group, using body shapes, spell out the name of the largest state? If you do not have enough people to spell the whole word, form as many letters as possible. [Alaska.] Can you use a different level to spell the second largest state? [Texas.] Use strong, muscular shapes to spell the third largest state. [California.] Can you use very small shapes to spell the smallest state in the Union? [Rhode Island.] Use small shapes again to spell the second smallest state. [Delaware.]

3. *(Divide the class into small groups.)* I am going to give each group a card on which the name of a state is written. Can you spell, with body shapes, the abbreviation of your state? When everyone is ready, we will watch each group and guess the name of the state from the abbreviation.

Variation: You may also reverse the process by giving the groups the abbreviation and asking them to spell the name of the state. Larger groups will be needed for this activity.

4. How quickly can you answer my questions by making the correct number with a body shape? Are you ready? How many states' names begin with the letter *A*? [4] Can you name them? How many states' names begin with the letter *B*? [0] How many begin with the letter *C*? [3] Can you name them?

Continue with the rest of the letters, and have the students name the states after making each letter. It is a good idea to have everyone make the correct number again after naming the states. This reinforces the right response. Instead of making body numbers, the children could touch body parts to the floor, put body parts on a high level or do nonlocomotor actions such as punch, stamp, clap, etc.

5. Can you describe some states' nicknames through movements? Can you show me Florida's nickname? [The Sunshine State.] Maine's nickname? [The Pine Tree State.] Texas's nickname? [Lone Star State.] West Virginia's nickname? [Mountain State.] Colorado's nickname? [Centennial State.]

Continue with other states. Discuss the meaning behind the nicknames of the states you are working on. This activity may also be done in groups with each group describing a nickname while the others try to guess the state associated with it.

6. Do you know the names of the original thirteen states? Let's go through them in the order of their admission to the Union. As I write each state's name on the board, make the abbreviation, one letter at a time, with body shapes.

7. Find a partner. I am going to ask you questions about landmarks, famous people, and events associated with certain states. Can each pair form the abbreviations of the states that answer the questions? What state is the home of Pikes Peak? [Col. or Colo.] Where did George Washington fight the battle of Trenton? [N.J.] Which state has four of the five Great Lakes touching its shores? [Mich.] Which state had a famous massacre and tea party? [Mass.] In which state did the Wright

Brothers have their first successful flight? [N.C.] Which state has the highest point of elevation? [Alas.]

Continue with similar questions. Variations: (a) Have groups or partners make up questions for other groups or partners to answer; (b) Have groups describe, through movement, landmarks, events, or famous people that are associated with certain states. Have other groups guess the dramatization and match it to the state.

8. *(Divide the class into groups of about seven people.)* I am going to give each group a card on which a state capital is written. Spell the capital with body shapes. If you do not have enough people to spell the whole word, form as many letters as you can. When everyone is ready we will look at the solutions, one at a time, and try to guess the state whose capital is being spelled.

   Variations: (a) Have the groups scramble the letters. The guessers must figure out the capital first and then name the state; (b) One group spells a state. The other group tries to spell its capital.

9. *(Divide the class into groups.)* Look at the map of the United States. Each group choose a state. Can you form the outline of your state by lying on the floor, head to toe? standing up with arms outstretched? sitting? kneeling? or by using a combination of these actions? Try several ways and choose one which you think is the clearest. When everyone is ready, we will look at each group and guess which state the group is making.

   Variations: (a) Have one person in each group make an interesting shape within the state outline at the place where the capital is located. The observers can guess the state and the capital. (b) Have the groups outline their states simultaneously and stand in the correct geographic relationship to each other.

10. Can you describe through movement some of the chief products of certain states? For what product is Idaho famous? [Potatoes.] Can you show me using body shapes and levels? What is one of Nebraska's chief products? [Corn.] What is an important product from Texas? [Oil.] from Mississippi?

[Cotton.] from Washington? [Apples and fish.] from Florida? [Oranges.] from West Virginia? [Coal.] *(Continue with other states.)*

11. *(Divide the class into two or three groups.)* Each group choose a state to research. Find out the capital, chief products, natural and man-made landmarks, famous people and events, size in area, and year of admission to the Union. After your research is completed, work together to produce a state pageant.

Describe your research through movement. You might form the outline of the state; then spell the capital, form numbers to show the rank in area and year of admission to the Union; depict some pertinent historic events; show the shapes of the chief products; and describe any important lakes, rivers, or mountains.

You may want to work together on every aspect or divide the research into different areas and ask certain group members to depict certain facts. However you decide to create your silent pageant, use the elements of movement to give variety and clarity to your actions.

This activity will take more than one class period to prepare. When a group is ready to show the results of its research, have the observers write down what they see and then try to name the state being depicted. Have the performers share their research and have the observers share their notes.

PART V

ART PROBLEMS

Shapes

Materials

Textures

Color

Symmetry

Asymmetry

Color

1. I am going to hold up some pieces of colored construction paper. Look at the color and react to that color through movement. How does the color make you feel? Maybe you associate the color with a particular object or place. Maybe it just brings a mood to mind. Move the way the color makes you feel. Use different levels, directions, speed, and force to help express your feelings. When I give the signal, stop and we will discuss your feelings.

   After the discussion, try several other colors. Discuss each. Stop each color improvisation before children run out of movement ideas. Twenty to thirty seconds is a good time limit.

2. Pick a color that you would like to work with. Look through magazines and find pictures using your color. Make a collage by pasting scraps of pictures that overlap each other all over a piece of paper.

   I will put these collages around the room. Now, let's divide into groups. Can your group pick a collage and create a dance to describe it? You might want to use the color, a picture on the collage, or shapes from the collage as your theme. We will watch the dances and see if we can guess which collage each group chose.

   Make the collages one day and do the dances another day.

3. Let us form two lines, shoulder-to-shoulder and facing each

257

How does the color yellow make you feel? Like dancing! ("Color," Problem 1)

other. I will stand behind one line and hold up a piece of colored paper. The line that can see the paper will try to make the opposite line guess the correct color. Use nonlocomotor movements to describe objects, moods, or places that represent the color you are looking at.

After one line guesses a color, I will stand behind the other line and hold up another color. We will keep guessing until I run out of colors.

4. Red, blue, and yellow are called *primary* colors. Green, orange, and purple are called *secondary* colors because they are made by putting two primary colors together. Red and blue make purple. Blue and yellow make green, and red and yellow make orange. *(Demonstrate this by mixing paints for the children.)*

Now, let's divide into six groups. Each group will represent one of the six colors we have talked about. I will give each of you a colored streamer so you can remember your color. Can the blues and yellows move around the room? Move with your streamers the way your color makes you feel. When I say "mix," find a person of the other color to dance with. When I say "melt," collapse to the floor and the secondary color of blue and yellow [*green*] get up and move.

Continue with yellow, red, and orange; then blue, red, and purple.

5. *(Divide the class into groups.)* I am going to give each group a card with a phrase on it. The phrases are about colors. Did you ever hear someone say, "He has a yellow streak"? What does that mean?

Now can you make up a movement phrase to illustrate the word phrase on your card? When your group is ready, sit down. We will watch each group and try to guess the color and phrase.

Some phrases you might use are: green with envy, red with embarrassment, red hot, icy blue, cool blue, in a blue mood, black as night, white as snow, born with a silver spoon in your mouth, good as gold, in the pink of health, in a brown study.

6. I am going to read some color poems from *Hailstones and Halibut Bones. (See Bibliography.)* As I read each poem slowly, listen to the color images and describe them through movement.

Variations: (a) Divide the class into groups. Let each group pick a color poem from which they can create a movement phrase. Have the groups perform for each other and let the audience guess each group's color. Encourage older children to focus in on one aspect of the poem. Have them explore that aspect in depth, or see if they can take one color image and create four different ways of presenting that image. (b) Use the poems as ideas for pictures. After the children have drawn their pictures, they can act them out.

7. *(Divide the class into groups.)* I am going to give each group a card with four or five objects of one color on it. Explore

movements for all the objects on your card; then choose one object for which you would like to create a movement phrase to perform for the class. We will try to guess your color and object.

For the color yellow you might use the sun, butter melting, wheat being cut, daffodils swaying in the breeze, and a candle flame flickering.

8. *Draw a simple design on paper using colors of the same mood such as red, oranges, and yellows or greens and blues.*

Look at the design on this paper. I am going to ask you questions but do not answer them out loud. Just think about the answer in your head. What level is the design on? What direction or directions does the design move in? Are the lines sharp or smooth? How do the colors affect you? Do they make you feel like moving slowly or quickly? Is the force of the design strong or weak? Now answer all those questions through movement. Can you dance the design? Let us try another one.

You might divide the class in half, have them watch each other, and discuss the different solutions.

9. *This problem should be done after working on Problem 8. Have the children make designs with crayons, paints, or paper as described in the previous problem.*

Can you translate your design into movement? How does your design make you want to move? *(After students have created short movement phrases, continue.)*

Now find a friend and trade designs. Study your friend's design and create a short movement phrase that describes the design. When you have finished, show each other the movement phrases you created. Did you friend's movement look anything like the movement you created for your design? What was different? What was the same? *(This can lead to a discussion of how people view art differently.)*

10. I am going to play a piece of music. Listen to the music for

Listen to the music and draw a design that describes how the music makes you feel. The music played for this design is obviously sad! ("Color," Problem 10)

awhile and then pick a colored crayon and draw a design. Let the music tell you what to draw and what colors to use.

Now I will play a second piece of music. *(It should be different in tempo and mood from the first one.)* Draw another design.

Let us look at the designs and talk a little bit about them. Can you tell to which piece of music this design was drawn? Why? What about this one? Why?

I will pick one design from the first set and one from the second. As I play the first music again, look at the design and move the way the design makes you feel. *(Repeat the activity with the second design.)*

Variation: Divide into groups. Let each group pick a design and create a movement phrase to compliment the design. Have the groups show the design dances to each other. Compare and contrast the artwork and the movement.

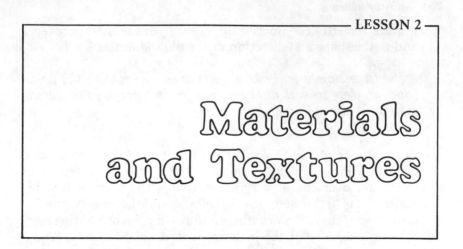

Materials and Textures

1. Find a partner. One of you be a mover and the other a painter. Can the mover create a short movement phrase and perform it for the painter? Can the painter describe the movement on paper? It is like drawing a portrait except that the painter is trying to capture the partner's movement, not the partner's physical likeness. Discuss the drawing and movement when you are finished and then change roles.

   To save time, both children could work on the movement phrases simultaneously and then take turns drawing.

2. *Divide the class into groups. This activity can be done at any grade level because the children do not have to work together within the group.*

   Can you form a living statue? Let's try. Group one stand over there. As I call out your name, run to this spot and freeze in an interesting shape. Each person in the group try to freeze on a different level and fill in an empty space. When everyone in the group is frozen, the rest of us will try to give a title to the statue we see.

   Variation: Make a mobile. Instead of freezing in a shape, the children stop in a shape but continue to move non-locomotorly, such as bouncing, stretching, twisting, etc.

3. I am going to be the artist and you will be my paint. Watch my brush strokes carefully. When I put my brush down, can you

263

imitate the strokes you saw by moving your body on the level and in the shape and direction my strokes indicated?

Make large simple arm movements in space for the children to follow. After several different designs, ask for a volunteer to take your place as artist.

4. *(Have the children bring in pieces of different textured material.)* Pick a piece of material that you like. Can you create a movement phrase that describes the texture of your material? Is it bumpy, rough, silky, smooth, ribbed, fluffy, heavy, scratchy? Besides the texture, try incorporating the pattern and color of the material into your movement. When everyone is ready, we will look at the movement phrases. Try to guess the material being described and give reasons for your guesses.

5. *Bring in large pieces of material such as a parachute, table-cloths or sheets, large plastic sheets, volleyball nets, tubular jersey, etc. Divide the class into groups.*

Each group pick a piece of material they would like to work with. Explore the material on different levels, with different directions, shape, range, speed, and force. Create a movement phrase that uses the material in three or four different ways. You might use it on three different levels, move it in four different directions, use it with the four qualities of force, move with it in three different speeds, or twist it around four different body shapes. These are just a few of the many ways to explore your material. We will look at your material designs when everyone is ready and discuss the elements of movement each group used.

Be sure each group has a chance to explore each piece of material at some time.

6. *Bring in yarn, string, or long pieces of elastic. Divide the class into groups.*

I am going to give each group a ball of yarn. Can each group construct a large, spatial three-dimensional yarn design? Use people to hold the yarn at different levels and in different

Can your group construct a three-dimensional yarn design? ("Materials and Textures," Problem 6)

places in space. Can your construction move and change shape without getting tangled up? Can members of your group move in and around the construction relating to it in many different ways? Let's watch each group.

Background music is helpful in motivating movement for this activity.

7. Find a partner. One of you will be a sculptor; the other will be a lump of clay. The sculptor will mold the clay into an interesting statue by moving one body part at a time into a shape. The sculptor can reshape any part. When the sculptor is finished, change roles so that the clay becomes the sculptor and vice versa. If you make a statue you really like, give it a title and remember its shape. You and your partner can show the statue to the class when we are through.

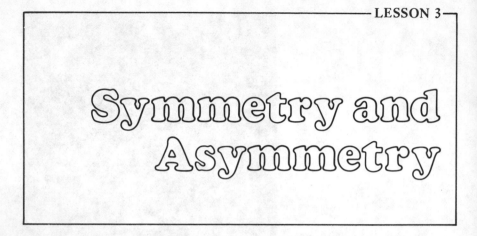

Symmetry and Asymmetry

1. Can you make a shape with your body that is symmetrical? If I cut your body in half and each side looked the same as the other, then your shape would be symmetrical. Try a symmetrical shape on a high level; on a medium level; on a low level. Can you make a symmetrical curved shape? a symmetrical angular shape? a symmetrical twisted shape? a symmetrical wide shape? a symmetrical narrow shape? Can you make a symmetrical shape with strong, tight muscles? with weak, loose muscles? Can you move your symmetrical shape through general space slowly? quickly? forewards? backwards? sideways?

2. Find a partner. Make a symmetrical shape with your partner. Can you make a symmetrical shape touching body parts? Can you make a symmetrical shape without touching? Try different levels. Try moving through space together. Let's look at some of the shapes and check the symmetry.

3. Find a partner. Stand opposite your partner. One of you will be your partner's mirror reflection. Follow everything your partner is doing just as though you were looking in a mirror. The leader must move slowly. Stay in your self space but try moving on different levels. When I give the signal, change leaders. Try moving as many different body parts as you can.

If the children are just moving their arms, ask them to put their arms behind them and try moving other body parts.

Divide the class in half so the children can look at the changing symmetrical shapes.

4. *(Divide the class into small groups.)* Form a symmetrical shape with your group. First try one touching body parts; then try one without touching. If we cut the group in half, each side should look the same. Now try another shape on a different level. Can you form a symmetrical shape with an odd number of people? [Yes.] Try one. Let's look at the shapes we've made.

5. *Have the children make Rorschach (ink) designs. Put a blob of ink or paint in the middle of a piece of paper pre-folded in half. Refold the paper and press down. Open up the paper and you should have a symmetrical design.*

Can you transcribe your ink design into a body shape? *(This can be done by individuals, in groups, or with partners.)*

Can you make a symmetrical shape with an odd number of people? According to these three, it's possible! ("Symmetry and Asymmetry," Problem 4)

Now trade designs with a friend and try making a shape similar to his or her design. Try adding nonlocomotor movement to your shape. What does the design remind you of? Can you keep the symmetrical shape but twist, bend, stretch, wiggle, turn, or bounce the way you think the design might if it were alive?

6. *(Divide the class into groups.)* Can each group create their own living, moving ink design? First make a symmetrical shape. Try to use different levels in your shape. Now mirror each other's movements. Can you think of a way to construct your design so that everyone doesn't move the same way but the design and movement remain symmetrical? *(Pairs within the group might do the same movement.)* When everyone is ready, we will look at the different designs.

7. Can you make an asymmetrical shape with your body? Asymmetry is just the opposite of symmetry. If I cut your body in half, each half will look different. Try using different levels; force; range; body shapes. Can you move your shapes through space in different directions? with different speeds?

8. *(Divide the class into small groups.)* Can you design a non-

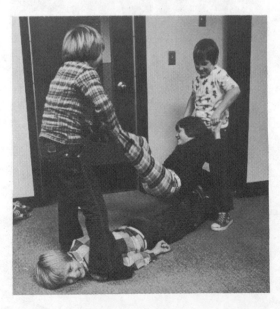

Can you make an asymmetrical shape with an even number of people? These four prove it can be done. ("Symmetry and Asymmetry," Problem 8)

moving asymmetrical design with your group? We will look at each design and give it a title just as we would a piece of art. Can you make an asymmetrical design with an even number of people? [Yes.] We will find out the answer when we look at the groups' solutions. Now, can you form a moving asymmetrical design?

9. *(Divide the class into groups.)* I am going to give each group a card with a movement problem written on it. Find a solution for your problem. When everyone is ready, we will look at each group and try to guess the group's problem by looking at the solution.

Give the following problems: (a) Form an asymmetrical design and move symmetrically; (b) Form a symmetrical design and move asymmetrically; (c) Form a symmetrical design and move symmetrically; (d) Form an asymmetrical design and move asymmetrically. You can give more than one group the same problem and discuss the different solutions the two groups design.

10. Use yarn, string, rope, paper streamers, or elastic to create a symmetrical three-dimensional design. Can you turn your design into a mobile and make it move either in its self space or through general space? Let's look at the designs. Now create an asymmetrical design. Which is harder to make: a symmetrical or an asymmetrical design? Why? *(Most children will say a symmetrical design because it is harder to create a perfectly balanced design than to create an unbalanced design.)*

Bibliography

Movement Education, Physical Education, and Related Arts

Anderson, Marian, et al. *Play with a Purpose*. New York: Harper & Row, 1966.
General physical education activities for grades K-8. Includes sections on movement exploration, dance skills, and good references.

Andrews, Gladys. *Creative Rhythmic Movement: Boys and Girls Dancing*. Englewood Cliffs, N.J.: Prentice-Hall, 1976.
An overall approach to creative movement and dance experiences. In addition to sound theory and methodology, there are specific suggestions for the use of songs, space, and rhythm in children's dance.

Andrews, Gladys, et al. *Physical Education for Today's Boys and Girls*. Boston: Allyn & Bacon, 1960.
A physical education text that focuses on creative aspects of dance for elementary school children. Includes both philosophy and practical ideas and resources.

Barlin, Anne, and Barlin, Paul. *The Art of Learning Through Movement*. Los Angeles: Ward Ritchie Press, 1971.
Contains creative movement activities for exploring space, time, and force. Geared for grades K-6. Simple, clear, and well illustrated.

Barrett, Kate. *Exploration—A Method for Teaching Movement*. Madison, Wis.: College Printing and Typing, 1965.
A manual that discusses the history and philosophy of movement exploration and presents practical lesson ideas.

Bilbrough, A., and Jones, P. *Physical Education in the Primary School.*
London: University of London Press, 1963.
A detailed and clear explanation of theory and teaching applications for
basic body movements; good description of the British approach to
movement education.

Boorman, Joyce. *Creative Dance in the First Three Grades.* New York:
David McKay, 1969.
Rudolf Laban's terminology and analysis of movement are used in this
book. While the importance of human movement as a means of expression
and exploration is stressed, practical ideas for the development of movement concepts are also provided.

————. *Creative Dance in Grades Four to Six.* Ontario: Longman Canada,
1971.
A companion book to *Creative Dance in the First Three Grades.* Includes
lesson plans.

Briggs, Megan M. *Movement Education: The Place of Movement in Physical
Education.* Boston: Plays, Inc., 1975.
Discusses movement as a basic approach to physical education. Deals
mainly with basic movement and educational gymnastics and offers
lesson ideas.

Brown, Margaret C., and Sommer, Betty K. *Movement Education: Its Evolu-
tion and a Modern Approach.* Reading, Mass.: Addison-Wesley, 1969.
Traces history of movement education and presents basic concepts and
teaching methods that emphasize exploration and discovery of sound and
natural movement. Gives exercise lessons divided into beginning, intermediate, and advanced skill levels.

Canner, Norma. *. . . And a Time to Dance.* Boston: Plays, Inc., 1975.
A simple and sensitive approach to teaching creative dance to young
children. Practical ideas are intermixed with philosophy and methodology.

Carr, Rachel. *Be a Frog, a Bird, or a Tree.* New York: Doubleday, 1973.
Inventive yoga exercises for children. Clear photographs of children
creating body forms that are descriptive of accompanying illustrations
and text.

Carroll, Jean, and Lofthouse, Peter. *Creative Dance for Boys.* London:
McDonald & Evans, 1969.
Contains five chapters with each taking an aspect of movement and
providing structured material for boys aged ten to sixteen. Material can
also be used in mixed class situations. Good photos.

Cratty, Bryant. *Active Learning: Games to Enhance Academic Abilities.* Englewood Cliffs, N.J.: Prentice-Hall, 1971.
Offers over 100 movement games that aid elementary learning processes. Suggests adjustments in games for use with retarded or handicapped children.

————. *Intelligence in Action: Physical Activities for Enhancing Intellectual Abilities.* Englewood Cliffs, N.J.: Prentice-Hall, 1973.
Offers practical, class-tested learning games that improve memory and analytical and synthetical abilities. Based on Piaget's cognition models.

————. *Learning about Human Behavior: Through Active Games.* Englewood Cliffs, N.J.: Prentice-Hall, 1975.
Games intended to make children more aware and understanding of different aspects of human behavior—friendship, cooperation, motivation, and individual differences. Games from other nations are also included.

Dauer, Victor P., and Pangrazi, Robert P. *Dynamic Physical Education for Elementary School Children.* Minneapolis: Burgess, 1975.
Good basic text for elementary physical education. Very useful chapter on movement education. Includes activities for perceptual-motor competency, gymnastics, and classroom games.

Dimondstein, Geraldine. *Children Dance in the Classroom.* New York: Macmillan, 1971.
Chapters on space, time, and force contain explanations of the terms followed by practical, structured material that explores the concept. Good photos and resource lists included.

Dorran, Margery, and Gulland, Frances. *Telling Stories through Movement.* Belmont, Calif.: Fearon Publishers, 1974.
Teaching suggestions and songs designed to accompany thirty well-known children's stories.

Furth, Hans, and Wachs, Harry. *Thinking Goes to School.* New York: Oxford University Press, 1974.
Discusses Piaget's theory of child development as it applies to learning situations. Of special interest is a practical section of movement and specific games that provide optimum learning environments.

Gallahue, David; Werner, Peter; and Luedke, George. *A Conceptual Approach to Moving and Learning.* New York: John Wiley & Sons, 1975.
Coordinates theories on the development of motor activity in children and how they learn through movement. Discusses how to teach these concepts at various grade levels.

Gerhardt, Lydia. *Moving and Knowing: The Young Child Orients Himself in Space.* Englewood Cliffs, N.J.: Prentice-Hall, 1973.
Deals with theory, but also offers practical suggestions to improve spatial discovery with children.

Gilbert, Celia. *International Folk Dance at a Glance.* Minneapolis: Burgess, 1969.
Provides basic dance steps and formations along with teaching suggestions. Emphasis is on mixers and dances without partners.

Gilliom, Bonnie. *Basic Movement Education for Children: Rationale and Teaching Units.* Reading, Mass.: Addison-Wesley, 1969.
Highly recommended as a basic text for movement education. Comprehensive discussion of movement education and the need for individualized teaching. Teaching units offered for three consecutive difficulty levels that use elements of movement and educational gymnastics.

Gray, Vera, and Percival, Rachel. *Music, Movement and Mime for Children.* New York: Oxford University Press, 1962.
Practical suggestions for guided movement exploration. Good pictures and music ideas.

Halsey, Elizabeth, and Porter, Lorena. *Physical Education for Children.* New York: Holt, Rinehart & Winston, 1963.
Emphasizes learning motor skills through movement exploration. Offers many problem examples that can be used practically.

Humphrey, James H. *Education of Children Through Motor Activity.* Springfield, Ill.: Charles C. Thomas, 1975.
Provides a sound, up-to-date overview of the theory and research on learning through motor activity. Also gives suggestions on coordinating motor activities with curriculum areas such as reading, mathematics, science, and social studies.

ICHPER Book of Worldwide Games and Dances. Washington, D.C.: American Alliance of Health, Physical Education & Recreation, 1967.
An anthology of sixty-eight games and thirty-nine dances from fifty-eight countries. Also includes music and diagrams.

Joyce, Mary. *First Steps in Teaching Creative Dance.* Palo Alto, Calif.: National Press Books, 1973.
Part I contains very clear, useful, and helpful material regarding method and theory. Part II contains fun, creative lesson plans that explore the elements of movement. Good photographs.

Kirchner, Glenn; Cunningham, Jean; and Warrell, Eileen. *Introduction to Movement Education: An Illustrated Program of Activities for Kindergarten through Grade Six.* Dubuque, Iowa: William C. Brown, 1974.
Good general text that discusses theories of physical education and movement as well as methods for teaching skills in a creative and exploratory manner. Offers lesson plans in addition to clear photographs and charts.

Laban, Rudolf. *Modern Educational Dance.* 2nd ed., rev. by Lisa Ullman. New York: Frederick A. Praeger, Publishers, 1963.
Theoretical explanation of rudiments of free dance technique and the sphere of movement.

Latchaw, Marjorie. *Human Movement: With Concepts Applied to Children's Movement Activities.* Englewood Cliffs, N.J.: Prentice-Hall, 1970.
Clearly presented study of the science of human movement. Includes practical ideas for movement activities as well. Explicit diagrams.

Montgomery, Chandler. *Art for Teachers of Children.* Columbus, Ohio: Charles E. Merrill Co., 1968.
Primarily focused on the visual arts, but there is also a good section that deals with movement and dance in terms of space, focus, and design.

Mosston, Muska. *Teaching Physical Education: From Command to Discovery.* Columbus, Ohio: Charles E. Merrill, 1966.
Carefully analyzes methods of instruction from the command style to the more individualized approach of creative problem solving. Offers useful classroom suggestions.

Murray, Ruth. *Dance in Elementary Education.* 2nd ed. New York: Harper & Row, 1963.
Comprehensive text that includes teaching techniques, creative activities, and traditional dance forms. Excellent chapters on locomotion, nonlocomotion, and rhythm that provide explanations and activities. Good reference materials and resource lists included.

North, Marion. *Movement Education: Child Development through Body Motion.* New York: E. P. Dutton, 1973.
History, theory, and practical lesson plans are provided by the author who is involved in British Primary School Movement Education.

Porter, Lorena. *Movement Education for Children: A New Direction in Elementary School Physical Education.* Washington, D.C.: American Association of Elementary, Kindergarten and Nursery Educators, 1969.
Provides history and definition of movement education. Especially useful for suggestions and for its annotated resource section on how to establish programs in movement education.

Sheehy, Erma. *Children Discover Music and Dance.* New York: Teacher's College Press, 1968.
Particularly important discussion regarding how to approach creative dance. Relates sound, listening to music, singing, and moving.

Sikes, Geraldine Brain. *Children's Literature for Dramatization.* New York: Harper & Row, 1964.
Collection of dramatic stories and poems with introductory statements on how children expressed this material.

Sloane, Eric. *Folklore of American Weather.* New York: Duell, Sloane and Pierce, 1963.
Contains many fascinating weather proverbs and anecdotes.

Sweeney, R. T., ed. *Selected Readings in Movement Education.* Reading, Mass.: Addison-Wesley, 1970.
Selections deal with three categories: "Theories of Movement," "Teacher and Methods," and "What is Movement Education." There is a large reference section.

Wickstrom, Ralph L. *Fundamental Motor Patterns.* Philadelphia: Lea & Febiger, 1970.
Chronological, developmental, and mechanical analysis of basic motor patterns as part of motor skill development: running, jumping, throwing, catching, kicking, and striking.

Useful Children's Books

General Series

Sesame Street Books, The. Boston: Little, Brown, 1969.
Five inventive books on numbers, puzzles, shapes, letters, and people and things.

Language Arts: Alphabet

Chwast, Seymour, and Moskof, Martin. *Still Another Alphabet Book.* New York: McGraw-Hill, 1969.
Picture-puzzle book that could inspire movement stories.

Fujikawa, Gyo. *A to Z Picture Book.* New York: Grosset & Dunlap, 1974.
Elaborate illustrations of children, animals, and objects relating to each letter of the alphabet. Beautifully colored pages alternate with black-and-white.

Geisel, Theodor Seuss (Seuss, Dr.). *On Beyond Zebra!* New York: Random House, 1955.
Fantastical alphabet letters accompanied by stories and illustrations of invented creatures.

Mendoza, George. *The Marcel Marceau Alphabet Book.* Garden City, N.Y.: Doubleday, 1970.
Full-page color photographs of Marcel Marceau portraying an image of whatever the alphabet letters inspire him to do.

Schmiderer, Dorothy. *The Alphabeast Book.* New York: Holt, Rinehart & Winston, 1971.
Alphabet letters are reshaped into three different forms until they approximate a living creature whose name begins with the letter.

Language Arts: Words

Gwynne, Fred. *The King Who Rained.* New York: Windmill Books and E. P. Dutton, 1970.
Marvelous story and illustrations of a child who discovers many confusing homophones.

Hoban, Tana. *Push, Pull, Empty, Full: A Book of Opposites.* New York: Macmillan, 1973.
Powerful and clear black-and-white photographs of situations or objects describing the antonyms chosen.

Language Arts: Literature

Aesop's Fables. Illustrated Junior Library Edition. New York: Grosset & Dunlap, 1947.
Collection of Aesop's fables, including "The Fox and the Crow."

Arbuthnot, May Hill, et al. *The Arbuthnot Anthology of Children's Literature.* 3rd ed. Glenview, Ill.: Scott Foresman, 1971.
Exceedingly comprehensive collection of poetry, folk tales, fables, myths, fiction, biography, and informational books. Extensive annotated bibliography.

Boegehold, Betty. *What the Wind Told.* New York: Parents Magazine Press, 1974.
Six fantastical stories told by the wind. Wonderful illustrations.

Borton, Helen. *Do You Move as I Do?* New York: Abelard-Schuman, 1963.
Focuses on action words and images from poetry and illustrations to inspire movement.

Brown, Marcia. *Once a Mouse: A Fable Cut in Wood.* New York: Charles Scribner's Sons, 1961.
The story of a hermit who changes a mouse into various animals. Extremely strong illustrations.

Ets, Marie Hall. *Gilberto and the Wind.* New York: Viking Press, 1963.
A Mexican boy discovers a new playmate—the wind. Expressive illustrations.

Grimm's Fairy Tales. Illustrated Junior Library Edition. New York: Grosset & Dunlap, 1945.
Collection of fairy tales by the Brothers Grimm.

Horwitz, Elinor Lander. *When the Sky Is Like Lace.* Philadelphia: J. B. Lippincott, 1975.
The adventures of three little girls written in vivid sound and movement words. Very expressive word images and illustrations.

Lamorisse, A. *Red Balloon.* Garden City, N.Y.: Doubleday, 1956.
The travels and adventures of a red balloon. Filmstrip also available.

Munari, Bruno. *The Circus in the Mist.* New York: World Publishing, 1968.
Inventively designed book about traveling through the mist in the city on the way to the dress rehearsal of a circus. Translucent pages with black, silhouetted city objects combine to give a realistic feeling of looking through the mist.

Sendak, Maurice. *Where the Wild Things Are.* New York: Harper & Row, 1963.
A little boy's imagination takes him on a trip to a place where monstrous creatures live who turn out to be very friendly. Charming illustrations.

Language Arts: Poetry

Adams, Adrienne, ed. *Poetry of the Earth.* New York: Charles Scribner's Sons, 1972.
Thirty-three poems by outstanding poets. The poems are simple but highly expressive in feeling, images, and movement.

Beilenson, Peter, trans. *Japanese Haiku.* Mount Vernon, N.Y.: Peter Pauper Press, 1955, 1956.
Two-hundred-twenty haiku by well-known Japanese poets.

Caudill, Rebecca. *Come Along.* New York: Holt, Rinehart & Winston, 1969.
Thirty haiku that reflect scenes or thoughts about nature.

Mendoza, George. *And I Must Hurry for the Sea Is Coming In.* Englewood Cliffs, N.J.: Prentice-Hall, 1969.
Poetry is used as an accompaniment to movement.

Sandburg, Carl. *The Carl Sandburg Treasury: Prose and Poetry for Young People.* New York: Harcourt Brace Jovanovich, 1970.
Includes the Abraham Lincoln stories, the "Rootabaga" stories, and two books of verse—*Early Moon* and *Wind Song.*

Specific Poems That Inspire Creative Movement

Note: In addition to citing the original editions in which these poems appeared, these entries cite the pages on which they appear in *The Arbuthnot Anthology of Children's Literature* (see bibliographical entry for Arbuthnot, May Hill, under Useful Children's Books—Language Arts: Literature).

Bacmeister, Rhoda. "Galoshes." In *Stories to Begin On.* New York: E. P. Dutton, 1940. *Arbuthnot,* p. 167.

Beyer, Evelyn. "Jump or Jiggle." In *Another Here and Now Story Book,* edited by Lucy Sprague Mitchell. New York: E. P. Dutton, 1937. *Arbuthnot,* p. 102.

Brown, Palmer, "The Spangled Pandemonium." In *Beyond the Paw Paw Trees.* New York: Harper & Row, 1954. *Arbuthnot,* p. 129.

De la Mare, Walter. "Seeds." In *Rhymes and Verses.* New York: Henry Holt, 1947. *Arbuthnot,* p. 202.

Fyleman, Rose. "The Goblin." In *Picture Rhymes from Foreign Lands.* New York: J. B. Lippincott, 1935. *Arbuthnot,* p. 152.

Hughes, Langston. "Long Trip." In *Selected Poems.* New York: Alfred A. Knopf, 1926. *Arbuthnot,* p. 97.

Kuskin, Karla. "Tiptoe." In *In the Middle of the Trees.* New York: Harper & Row, 1958. *Arbuthnot,* p. 102.

Lowell, Amy, "The City of Falling Leaves." From "1777" in *Men, Women and Ghosts.* Boston: Houghton-Mifflin. *Arbuthnot,* p. 184.

Milne, A. A. "Hoppity." In *When We Were Very Young.* New York: E. P. Dutton, 1924. *Arbuthnot,* p. 100.

Sandburg, Carl. "Fog." In *Chicago Poems.* New York: Henry Holt, 1916. *Arbuthnot,* p. 171.

_____. "Grass Roots." In *The Carl Sandburg Treasury*. New York: Harcourt Brace Jovanovich, 1970. *Arbuthnot*, p. 250.

Stephens, James. "Check." In *Rocky Road to Dublin*. New York: Macmillan, 1915. *Arbuthnot*, p. 178.

Stevenson, Robert Louis. "Marching Song." In *A Child's Garden of Verses*. *Arbuthnot*, p. 112.

_____. "My Shadow." In *A Child's Garden of Verses*. *Arbuthnot*, p. 112.

_____. "The Swing." In *A Child's Garden of Verses*. *Arbuthnot*, p. 107.

Mathematics

Atwood, Ann. *The Little Circle*. New York: Charles Scribner's Sons, 1967.
Focuses on the circle in nature and how all or parts of the body can make circles.

Froman, Robert. *Bigger and Smaller*. New York: Thomas Y. Crowell, 1971.
Nicely illustrated with many thought-provoking facts about large and small objects and creatures.

Heide, Florence, and Van Cleif, Sylvia. *How Big Am I*. Chicago: Follett, 1968.
Uses comparisons and therefore can aid in exploring big-little concepts.

Hoban, Tana. *Circles, Triangles, and Squares*. New York: Macmillan, 1974.
Black-and-white photographs show everyday objects or situations in such a way that the underlying geometry is readily perceivable.

_____. *Over, Under and Through*. New York: Macmillan, 1973.
Black-and-white photographs show children acting out these spatial concepts using ordinary, familiar objects.

_____. *Shapes and Things*. New York: Macmillan, 1970.
Black-and-white photographs of everyday items express shape so well that they can easily be translated into body movements.

Lionni, Leo. *Inch by Inch*. New York: Astor-Honor, 1960.
Helps develop measuring concepts through use of the body.

Mendoza, George. *The Marcel Marceau Counting Book*. Garden City, N.Y.: Doubleday, 1971.
Color photographs of Marcel Marceau wearing twenty different hats as he depicts twenty different professions.

Robinson, Shari. *Numbers, Signs, and Pictures.* New York: Platt & Munk, 1975.
Counting and mathematical operations through division are depicted in hilarious situations. Clever and clear illustrations.

Schlein, Miriam. *Shapes.* New York: William R. Scott, 1964.
Suggestions that inspire the invention and movement of body shapes in space.

Science

Brandy, Franklyn. *Gravity is a Mystery.* New York: Thomas Y. Crowell, 1970.
Discusses gravity simply and clearly.

Brown, M. W. *Good-Night Moon.* New York: Harper & Row, 1948.
Charming opportunity for identifying objects and feeling close to nature.

Geisel, Theodor Seuss (Seuss, Dr.). *Bartholomew and the Oobleck.* New York: Random House, 1949.
Delightful story about weather. The king is tired of the same four things coming down on him—snow, fog, sunshine, and rain—so the magicians bring down Oobleck.

Kuskin, Karla. *All Sizes of Noises.* New York: Harper & Row, 1962.
Familiarizes children with the variety of sounds people make.

Lipton, James. *An Exaltation of Larks.* New York: Grossman Publishers, 1968.
Presents a collection of enchanting illustrations of animals in addition to the group names of each species.

O'Neill, Mary. *Winds.* Garden City, N.Y.: Doubleday, 1970.
Poems about the different moods of the wind.

Parsley, Mary, ed. *My Book of Stories for All Seasons.* New York: Larousse, 1972.
Thirty-six stories that conjure up feelings appropriate to each of the four seasons.

Rey, H. A. *The Stars.* Boston: Houghton-Mifflin, 1970.
Shows how to see different designs made by stars.

Rockwell, Anne. *Machines.* New York: Macmillan, 1972.
Bright and bold watercolor illustrations of machines. Clear statements of how machines work and what powers them.

Social Studies

Burton, Virginia Lee. *Mike Mulligan and His Steam Shovel*. Boston: Houghton-Mifflin, 1939.
This story is particularly useful because of the dynamic personification of the steam shovel.

Gaer, Joseph. *Holidays around the World*. Boston: Little, Brown, 1953.
Includes Chinese, Hindu, Moslem, Hebrew, and Christian holidays and discusses origins, customs, and legends.

Ickis, Marguerite. *The Book of Festival Holidays*. New York: Dodd, Mead, 1964.
Includes origins of holidays, customs, art ideas and crafts, games, songs, and dances related to them.

————. *The Book of Patriotic Holidays*. New York: Dodd, Mead, 1962.
Includes anecdotes, arts and crafts, and other activities related to patriotic holidays.

Kraus, Richard. *Folk Dancing*. New York: Macmillan, 1962.
Includes European and American folk dances. Basic positions, formations, skills, and steps are illustrated by diagrams.

Nickerson, Betty. *Celebrate the Sun*. New York: J. B. Lippincott, 1969.
Presents background of festivals as seen through children's art from all over the world. Also related to ethnic dance.

O'Neill, Mary. *People I'd Like to Keep*. Garden City, N.Y.: Doubleday, 1964.
Wonderful images, words, and honest descriptions of people like the grade school principal, the doctor, circus people, and "Uggle" (the blanket).

Peet, Bill. *The Wump World*. Boston: Houghton-Mifflin, 1970.
A book of crayon drawings that warn about the dangers of pollution all over the world.

Scarry, Richard. *Cars and Trucks and Things That Go*. New York: Golden Press, 1974.
Numerous color drawings of real vehicles (often personified in feeling) and imaginary vehicles (the shoe delivery car in the shape of a shoe).

Wildsmith, Brian. *Circus*. New York: Franklin Watts, 1970.
Spectacular illustrations that easily inspire circus movements.

Zolotov, C. *Over and Over*. New York: Harper & Row, 1957.
Chronological presentation of holidays that ends in a birthday party.

Art

Bond, Jean Carey. *Brown Is a Beautiful Color.* New York: Franklin Watts, 1969.
Life of a city child in poetry.

Charosh, Mannes. *Straight Lines, Parallel Lines, Perpendicular Lines.* New York: Thomas Y. Crowell, 1970.
Discussion of lines can be transferred to body movements and floor patterns.

Johnson, Crockett. *Harold and the Purple Crayon.* New York: Harper & Row, 1955.
Fantastical adventures can easily be translated to movement.

Klee, Paul. *Pedagogical Sketchbook.* New York: Frederick A. Praeger Publishers, 1953.
This treatise by the artist on the principles of visual art is readily approachable on the less complex level of his whimsical drawings and doodlings. Line and shape is shown as growing, dynamic expression rather than merely static symbol.

Lionni, Leo. *Little Blue and Little Yellow.* New York: McDowell, Obolensky, 1959.
Abstract, personified shapes of blue and yellow get together to form green and then separate again. Film also available.

McAgy, D. E. *Going for a Walk with a Line.* Garden City, N.Y.: Doubleday, 1959.
Deals in various ways with the concept of line and aids in expanding children's awareness of what they see.

O'Neill, Mary. *Hailstones and Halibut Bones: Adventures in Color.* Garden City, N.Y.: Doubleday, 1961.
Twelve poems that relate color to sound, taste, smell, touch, sight, and feelings. Film also available.

Sitomer, Mindel, and Sitomer, Harry. *What is Symmetry?* New York: Thomas Y. Crowell, 1972.
Presents examples of symmetry in nature and the manufactured environment. Filmstrip also available.

Tison, Annette, and Taylor, Talus. *The Adventures of the Three Colors.* New York: World, 1971.
The adventures of Herbie who has only three colors—blue, yellow, and pink—in his paint box. Designed with transparent pages allowing color overlay so that new colors and shapes appear when pages are superimposed.

Music

Boni, Margaret B., and Lloyd, N. *Favorite American Songs.* New York: Simon and Schuster, 1956.
Historical selection of American songs from the Revolutionary War through the turn of the century.

————. *Fireside Book of Folk Songs.* New York: Simon and Schuster, 1947.
International selection of folk songs including Christmas carols.

Brown, Margaret W. *The Quiet Noisy Book.* New York: Harper & Row, 1950.
Amusing book that asks repeated questions about what woke up the dog. All the answers are soundless or impossible (a bee wondering) and are presented in a very loud four-color format.

Fowke, Edith. *Sally Go Round the Sun.* Garden City, N.Y.: Doubleday, 1969.
Over 300 songs, rhymes, and games from backyard, school recess, and street corner heritage. Includes foot and finger plays, and number rhymes.

Grayson, Marion. *Let's Do Finger Plays.* Washington, D.C.: Robert B. Luce, 1962.
Old and recent songs and poems for finger plays. Line-by-line teacher directions.

Hansen, Charles, ed. *400 Super Song Fest: Folk Songs of Today.* New York: Folk World, 1973.
Very complete anthology of folk songs. Includes "Dry Bones," p. 57.

Miller, Carl S., ed. *Sing, Children, Sing.* New York: Chappell, 1972.
Singing games and songs from all over the world.

Poulsson, Emilie. *Fingerplays for Nursery and Kindergarten.* New York: Dover, 1971.
Eighteen fingerplays to be done to poems and songs. Republication of an 1893 edition, complete with original illustrations of finger positions.

Whitman, Wanda W., ed. *Songs that Changed the World.* New York: Crown, 1969.
Songs about patriotism, war, hard times, escape, religion, and politics that inspired emotions.

Winn, Marie, ed. *Fireside Book of Children's Songs.* New York: Simon and Schuster, 1966.
Includes animal songs, silly songs, singing games, and rounds. Includes "The Hokey Pokey," p. 168.

Classroom Psychology and Management

Dreikurs, Rudolph. *Psychology in the Classroom: A Manual for Teachers.* 2nd ed. New York: Harper & Row, 1968.
Contains real-life examples of problems encountered in the classroom and offers practical ways of handling these situations positively.

Ginott, Haim. *Between Parent and Child.* New York: Macmillan, 1965.
Practical suggestions for communicating positively and effectively with children.

_____. *Between Teacher and Child.* New York: Macmillan, 1972.
Offers new solutions to old problems.

Glasser, William. *Schools without Failure.* New York: Harper & Row, 1969.
Contains creative ideas for providing more successful experiences in our schools. The chapters on handling group discussion are particularly valuable.

Gordon, Thomas. *T.E.T. Teacher Effectiveness Training.* New York: Peter H. Wyden, Publisher, 1974.
A system for parents and teachers that is aimed at teaching better communication skills, modifying the classroom environment to prevent problems, and resolving conflicts through positive methods. Very practical and useful ideas.

Holt, John. *How Children Fail.* New York: Pitman, 1964.
An examination of children's failures in school based on years of observation as a teacher.

_____. *How Children Learn.* New York: Pitman, 1967.
A penetrating examination of American mores and education.

Krumboltz, John, and Krumboltz, Helen. *Changing Children's Behavior.* Englewood Cliffs, N.J.: Prentice-Hall, 1972.
Over 150 examples, based on actual events, show what adults can do to help children learn, strengthen existing behavior, develop and maintain new behavior, and stop inappropriate behavior. Well indexed. Clear and very helpful.

Neill, A. S. *Summerhill.* New York: Hart, 1960.
Termed by many as a radical approach to child rearing, Neill's school in England provides unusual learning experiences for children. A provocative reading experience for adults.

Postman, Neil, and Weingartner, Charles. *Teaching as a Subversive Activity.*
New York: Delacorte Press, 1969.
This book helped bring about the present awareness of the need for better
teaching methods in our schools. A must for teachers wanting to provide
a democratic atmosphere and more meaningful experiences for their
students.

Rogers, Carl. *Freedom to Learn.* Columbus, Ohio: Charles E. Merrill, 1969.
Contains philosophy mixed with practical ideas on how to create an
atmosphere where positive learning can thrive.

Recordings

Activity Songs for Kids. Scholastic Records, SC7523.
Songs for Halloween and songs about machines, animals, and boats.
Booklet included.

All-Purpose Folk Dances. RCA, LPM 1623.
Includes "Bingo," "Cherkassiya," "Seven Jumps." Instructions included.

American Games and Activity Songs for Children. Pete Seeger. Folkways/
Scholastic, FC 7002.

Carnival of the Animals. Saint-Saens. Columbia, MS 6368.
Narrated by Leonard Bernstein. Can be used for creative animal imitations.

Children's Corner Suite. Debussy. Columbia, MS 6567.
Good melodies and rhythm for improvisation.

Come Dance with Me. Virginia Tanner. Hoctor Educational Records, HLP
3078.
Inspiring music with titles such as "Words that Rhyme." One record with
narration; one with just music. Tempo, rhythmic patterns, skip, and
qualities of force are explored.

Dance-A-Story. Anne Barlin. RCA, LE 101-108.
Eight albums with a companion story book included in each album.
Stories are about such topics as balloons, Noah's ark, toy tree, and a
little duck.

Danse Macabre. Saint Saens. Many recordings available.
Mysterious, spooky music excellent for Halloween improvisations.

Electronic Record for Children. Dimension 5, E-141.
Narrated electronic music of much variety with such suggestive titles as
"Upside Down."

Environments. Atlantic, SD66001.
One side features a recording of waves for rocking, rolling, and resting. The other side features a recording of an aviary.

Four Swinging Seasons. Capitol International, SP 10547.
Jazz version of Vivaldi's "Four Seasons."

Hap Palmer Record Library. Educational Activities Inc.: Freeport, N.Y. 11520.
Sixteen albums which can be ordered separately. Titles include "Learning Basic Skills through Movement," "The Feel of Music," and "Holiday Songs and Rhythms," among others. Albums feature enjoyable music and songs with a modern sound. Suggested movement activities included on record jacket.

Hokey Pokey. MacGregor, 45 rpm, 6995.
Comes with printed calling instructions.

Listen and Move Series. McDonald and Evans, Ltd., 8 John St., London, W.C.1.
Four records presenting simple to more difficult rhythms. Follows Laban's movement theory.

Music for Rhythms and Dance. Freda Miller Records for Dance, 131 Bayview Ave., Northport, N.Y. 11768. Vol. 4.
Excellent for dramatic movement, compositions, emotions, and locomotor skills.

Nonesuch Explorer, Music from Distant Corners of the World. Nonesuch Records, H7-11.
Two-record set. Good background music for improvisations and for social studies units on cultures.

Piano Music of Erik Satie. Angel Records, S 36714, Vol. 4.
Good background music for improvisations.

Play Your Instruments and Make a Pretty Sound. Ella Jenkins. Folkway Records, FC 7665.
Excellent songs and activities for rhythm band and movement.

Rhythms of the World. Langston Hughes. Folkways Records, FC 7340.
Discusses numerous rhythms from nature such as heart-beat sounds and animal sounds. Booklet included.

Songs to Grow On. Woody Guthrie. Folkways Records, FC 7005.
Fun songs to inspire dance. Booklet included.

Sounds of . . . Science Series. Folkways Records.
Sounds of animals, steam locomotives, science fiction, and patterns.

Space Songs. Motivation Records, Division of Argosy Music Corp., MR 0312.
A singing science record.

Square Dance Book and Record, Do-si-do and away we go. Wonderland
Records/AA Records, GST-15.
Includes "Looby Lou."

Way-Out Record for Children, The. Dimension 5 Records. Stereo # D-131.
Features unusual sounds and electronic effects. Music with and without
narration. Particularly good for intermediate grades.

Films

Art and Motion. Encyclopedia Britannica Educational Corp.: 17 min., color.
Can be used to motivate movement inspired by the natural environment.

Balance. Ealing Corp., 1969: 4 min., silent, color, super 8mm.
Shows children balancing alone or together on various body parts.

Children Dance. University of California Extension Media Center, 1970:
14 min., black-and-white.
Time, force, space, and dance imagery explored by children, grades K-3.
Produced by Geraldine Dimondstein and Naima Prevots.

Dance Squared. International Film Bureau, 1963: 4 min., color.
Emphasizes symmetry of the square. Can motivate floor patterns and
relationships.

Flow of Movement. Ealing Corp., 1969: 4 min., silent, color, super 8mm.
Connects separate parts of action into continuous pattern.

Force of Movement. Ealing Corp., 1969: 4 min., silent, color, super 8mm.
Illustrates concepts of weak, light, strong, and heavy.

Hailstones and Halibut Bones (Parts I and II). Sterling Educational Films,
1964-67: 6 and 8 min., color.
Poems are selected from book of the same title and are accompanied by
colors that express the feelings intended.

Images from Nature. Indiana University Audio-Visual Center, 1962: 7 min.,
color.
Scenes from natural environment that correspond with the seasons.
Animations also.

Learning Through Movement. SL Productions, 1960: 30 min., Black-and-white.
Shows boys and girls of various ages engaged in the activities described in the book of the same name.

Little Blue and Little Yellow. Contemporary Films/McGraw-Hill, 1962: 11 min., color.
As the book of the same title, this film teaches the primary colors. Could motivate a three-part dance.

Looking for Me. University of California Extension Media Center, 1971: 29 min., black-and-white.
Shows importance of body movement and self-awareness with normal and autistic children.

Moving at Different Levels. Ealing Corp., 1969: 3 min., silent, color, super 8mm.
Direction related to moving at different levels.

Moving in Many Directions. Ealing Corp., 1969: 4 min., silent, color, super 8mm.
Illustrates six directions of possible movement.

Movement in Time and Space. Peter M. Rodeck & Co., 1950s: 30 min., black-and-white. Rental available from University of California Extension Media Center.
Shows children in British primary school exploring movement problems. At the conclusion, children present dance version of "Jabberwocky," inventing their own sound effects and words. Part of a BBC series filmed in the 1950s.

Movements: Fast and Slow. Ealing Corp., 1969: 4 min. silent, color, super 8mm.
Combines changes in speed with changes in level and directions.

Movements: Large and Small. Ealing Corp., 1969: 4 min., silent, color, super 8mm.
Complete range of movement from curling to extension.

Once Upon a Time There Was a Dot. Contemporary Films/McGraw-Hill, 1967: 8 min., color.
Animation of a dot changing into various objects such as an airplane and a musical instrument.

Yarn, Balls, Hoops, Ropes, and Wands. Ealing Corp., 1969: 3 min., silent, color, super 8mm.

Stresses control, balance, moving over and under, and working with others.

Film Distributors

Contemporary Films/McGraw-Hill (CMH), 330 W. 42nd St., New York, N.Y. 10036.

Ealing Corp., 2225 Massachusetts Ave., Cambridge, Mass. 02140.

Encyclopedia Britannica Education Corp., 425 N. Michigan Ave., Chicago, Ill. 60611.

Indiana University Audio-Visual Center, Bloomington, Ind. 47401.

International Film Bureau, 332 S. Michigan Ave., Chicago, Ill. 60604.

Rodeck & Co., Peter M., 230 Park Ave., New York, N.Y. 10017.

SL Productions, P. O. Box 41108, Los Angeles, Calif. 90041

Sterling Educational Films, 241 E. 34th St., New York, N.Y. 10016.

University of California Extension Media Center, Berkeley, Calif. 94720.

Index

291